Second Chance for Life

Jesus said, "If? There are no ifs among believers. Anything can happen."

—Mark 9:23(MSG)

Second Chance for Life

Empowering Yourself to Heal Body, Mind & Spirit

Wally Hogland

Second Chance for Life

Empowering Yourself to Heal Mind, Body & Spirit

Manufactured in the United States of America.

For information, please contact:

The P3 Press
16200 North Dallas Parkway, Suite 170
Dallas, Texas 75248

www.thep3press.com

972-248-9500

A New Era in Publishing™

Hardbound ISBN-13: 978-1-933651-44-6
Hardbound ISBN-10: 1-933651-44-X
Paperback ISBN-13: 978-1-933651-45-3
Paperback ISBN-10: 1-933651-45-8
LCCN: 2008907735

Author contact information:

Wally Hogland

www.wallyhogland.com

Scripture quotations marked NLT are taken from the Holy Bible, New Living Translation, copyright 1996, 2004. Used by permission of Tyndale House Publishers, Inc., Wheaton, Illinois 60189. All rights reserved.

Dedication

To my spiritual heavenly Father, who made me, blessed me, and lives in me forever—all praise and glory to him.

To my beloved friends Mr. and Mrs. A.C. Houser who have long since passed on to their reward but not without leaving me the inspiration to help others and to believe in being the best Christian I can be. I will remember and love you always.

To my father, Ward Hogland, who taught me knowledge of the Bible to give me comfort and provide a compass for my life. I never met a person more knowledgeable about God's Word or able to explain it like my father. Thank you, Father, for your time, patience, and encouragement.

To my mother, Maxine Hogland, who gave me the determination of a tenacious bulldog to never give up. That determination helped to save my life. Thanks, Mom.

To my beloved wife, Mary Beth, who has stood so steadfastly by my side. I could not have written this book without you, my love. Thank you!

To my son, Brandon, you have been a major inspiration to me to live and to have a second chance for life. You have always been a blessing in my life and I thank God for you on a daily basis. I will always love you.

Contents

Preface

I was motivated to write *Second Chance for Life* while I was going through a grueling regimen of radiation therapy. At the hospital, I was witness to an overwhelming lack of hope among the countless patients and their families who were torn apart by cancer diagnoses and treatments.

I knew that the Creator of the universe never intended for mankind to live in such endless fear, despair, and frustration. God intended for us all to have joy, victory, success, and happiness. He is the source of all hope.

I realized I had a gift of being able to offer a glimpse of that hope to others, no matter how dark their paths seemed. I wrote this book through the process of my own prayerful healing through faith. I dug into God's Word and applied it to my life and my broken situation. I was able to find light in the darkness surrounding me and was lifted up into wellness to share with others hope through the story of my miraculous recovery.

My desire is for this book to bring back the reader's awareness of the passion God always wanted us to live with and to remind the reader of how important our mission is on earth. We each have a divine purpose; these trials and tribulations can be used to lift us up out of the mire and plant our feet back on that path of joy.

I've written this book to share the hope I've found, but it is in no way a prescription for you or your loved one. Any statement in this book, *Second Chance for Life*, is based upon my own recovery. Anyone with health issues should consult with professional medical doctors. Results may vary from human to human, since all are not identical. Answers, comments, and opinions provided in *Second Chance for Life* are general information, and are not intended to substitute for informed professional medical, psychiatric, psychological, or other professional advice. You should always speak with your physician or a healthcare professional before taking any medication; or nutritional, herbal, or homeopathic supplement; or adopting any treatment for a health problem.

May you find your second chance for life.

Wally Hogland

One

Facing Adversity, No Denial

I have lived through adversity:

1. In 1999 I had a stroke that consisted of a right brain bleed. Doctors did not give me much hope.
2. In 2002 I lost my job and was laid off at Christmas.
3. In 2003 I discovered that I had cancer. It was advanced stage IV. My doctors did not give me much hope.

The miracle? I am still here! Alive! With an active brain, a new job, and I am cancer free!

I wish to share with those of you who are also facing adversity my sense of hope and the sources of healing and comfort I discovered in the toughest moments of my life.

When my doctor came in and told me that he had bad news, I had cancer—advanced stage IV cancer—my mind descended into a deep, dark pit. My wife sat in a corner of the room, tears running down her face. At the time she thought, Could this be the end of Wally's life?

One of my friends later remarked, "It is as if a dragon showed up at my door and I had no defense against it."

As I pondered my fate, I went through many emotions: despair, anger, anxiety, humility, frustration, fear, denial, and confusion. I am sure you can relate and understand if you have been or are going through similar circumstances. That evening I did not sleep much at all, tormenting my mind over what I discovered. I rose before the sun was up and prepared myself for the day. I started my day off by walking my dog, Sam, a Boston terrier bulldog that I love very much.

As Sam and I walked the neighborhood in the early morning hours, I noticed things that I had never paid much attention to. My life-and-death situation left my mind more acute than it had ever been. I gazed up at the stars, in awe of their beauty and majesty. I could no longer take for granted one second of life. I appreciated the fresh morning air and the energy it gave to me. As my mind started down this path of awareness, I pictured my life and realized that I had not fulfilled my purpose. **I needed a second chance for life.** I know I am not the only one out there who has faced such a moment of despair. We all need grace, mercy, and kindness. We all need second chances.

That morning, as my footsteps echoed on concrete and the smell of morning dew on the grass filled my nostrils with the scent of a new day beginning, I came to a resolution.

I was starting my own new day. I would fight this decree that I was going to die.

I communicated and reconciled myself with God that morning in the most sincere manner I knew how, pleading my case before the Lord. I knew I had no control over my situation and went to the only power that could truly help me. I knew I was going to die someday, but NOT NOW! I made a commitment to fight to live. I had the strongest motivation a father could have, in an eight-year-old son and a beautiful wife that needed me! I refused to accept the diagnosis the doctors had prescribed for me and decided to come up with my own—a second chance for life!

I revised and rededicated myself to my belief system that morning. With God at my side, I knew that all good things were possible for those who believe.

I made a commitment to live.

I promised God that when I was successful, I would help and serve others that were going through what I was going through. I am a living testimony to that commitment today. The reason I am alive today is because of the grace, mercy, and love of the Almighty God, and because I had faith in, and sought to understand, the messages that God gave me. You may be asking: But why you, Wally? Others have gone through what you have and not lived. What makes you special? I am not special, just blessed, which is something anyone can have from their eternal source.

I am going to let the reader in on the messages God gave me to conquer my adversities.

First, let's clearly define the word **adversity**. Adversity to some people is just simply bad luck. In other words, bad things happen because you are just a victim of circumstance.

When I speak of adversity, I am talking about a very profound event, a dead end with **no hope.** At least that is what we are led to believe. *The Foolish Dictionary* of 1904 describes adversity as being a "bottomless lake, surrounded by near-sighted friends." This clearly describes the story of Job's adversity, and of my own. Job was on top of the world one day, and suddenly everything he had was gone, including his health!

Words from the Wise

"Adversity is the diamond dust that Heaven polishes its jewels with."

—Thomas Carlyle

"Fire is the test of gold; adversity, of strong men."

—Martha Graham

"Show me someone who has done something worthwhile, and I will show you someone who has overcome adversity."

—Lou Holtz

"Adversity often pushes us into our divine destiny."

—Joel Osteen, *Your Best Life Now*

We must come to terms with adversity and realize that a crisis is not necessarily a bad thing, but it can be used as a powerful tool to make us more than we could ever imagine.

I learned not to fight or deny adversity. I learned to embrace it with God's help. As my doctors decided on a treatment for my cancer, I was discovering a healthy way for my mind, body, and spirit to face my changed future.

I am not saying that you should go out and find adversity. But when it does come into your life, put it in the proper context and allow your divine creator to help you with all of your life challenges.

Healing Scriptures

God has not given us a **spirit of fear, but of power, and of love, and of sound mind.**

2 Timothy 1:7 (NKJV)

When you go through deep waters and great trouble,
I will be with you. When you go through rivers of difficulty,
you will not drown.

Isaiah 43:2 (TLB)

Rejoice in the Lord always. I will say it again: Rejoice!
Let your gentleness be evident to all. **The Lord is near.**
Do not be anxious about anything, but in everything,
by prayer and petition, with thanksgiving, present your
requests to God. And the peace of God, which transcends
all understanding, will guard your hearts and
your minds in Christ Jesus.

Philippians 4:4–7 (NIV)

God can pour on the blessings in astonishing ways
so that you're ready for anything and everything, more than
just ready to do what needs to be done.

2 Corinthians 9:8 (MSG)

Give your entire attention to what God is doing
right now, and don't get worked up about what may or
may not happen tomorrow. **God will help you deal with**
whatever hard things come up when the time comes.

Matthew 6:34 (MSG)

See, **I am sending an angel ahead of you to guard** you along the way and to bring you to the place I have prepared. … Worship the LORD your God, and **his blessing will be on your food and water. I will take away sickness . . . and I will give you a full life span.**

Exodus 23:20–27 (NIV)

The Lord is my strength and my song;
he has become my Salvation.

Exodus 15:2 (NIV)

When swimming in the ocean, one must be aware of rip currents. These powerful forces of nature can pull a swimmer out to sea and leave the swimmer exhausted, tired, and frustrated, and even good swimmers can drown. Lifeguards, who try to assist when the swimmer is still fighting, can be pulled under by the swimmer who fights to control his own destiny. It is only when the swimmer surrenders, allowing the lifeguard to take charge, that the two make it safely to shore. In like manner, until we surrender to adversity and do not deny its grip upon us, realizing that we are not in control, only then can we truly call upon our creator to help us in our time of need.

Steps I Used to Heal My Body and My Mind

- I recognized the beauty of my life
- I realized I had not fulfilled my purpose
- I resolved to fight
- I pled my case to the Lord
- I made a commitment to live
- I dedicated myself to surviving
- I vowed to help and serve others in the same struggle
- I surrendered myself to God

Two

Why Me? What Do I Do Now?

I began asking questions:

1. Why had these terrible adversities come into my life?
2. Was God trying to talk to me?
3. Did God want me to do something else with my life?
4. Do I have choices to make?
5. Do I have any control of my life?

It is not easy to surrender a personal crisis to the Lord. I have to admit I kept asking *Why me?* But I opened up my mind, heart, and spirit to the Lord's help in facing adversity. I was seeking answers. The Lord says, "Seek and you will find," (Matt. 7:7 NIV). I truly believe this because it wasn't until I was seeking answers that I started finding them. I began to recognize when God sent me answers. I became aware of God's involvement in my life.

"If you **call out for insight** and **cry aloud for understanding,** and if you look for it as for silver and search for it as for hidden treasure, then you will understand the fear of the LORD and **find the knowledge of God."**

Proverbs 2:3–5 (NIV)

I was waiting on my little boy to get out of school on the day God turned the tables on me and taught me a lesson. The tool God used to reach me was the Christian bookstore at the school. Imagine my surprise when the first title to catch my eyes on the CD rack was a recorded sermon entitled "If the Lord Is with Us, Why Has All This Happened to Me?"

WOW! Was God talking to me?

I purchased the CD by Dr. O.S. Hawkins and listened to it on the way home with intense interest. I was blown away. The sermon Dr. Hawkins had recorded brought me comfort throughout the coming weeks, again and again, as my cancer treatments began. The scripture Dr. Hawkins quoted that spoke to me directly was:

> "We were under great pressure, far beyond our ability to endure, so that we despaired even of life. Indeed, in our hearts we felt the sentence of death. But this happened that **we might not rely on ourselves but on God,** who raises the dead."
>
> **2 Corinthians 1:9 (NIV)**

I was under pressure. I despaired of life. I felt the sentence of death.

Had this cancer happened that I might rely on God?

I saw a parallel between Paul's circumstances and mine. When I was lying on my bed in the hospital, I took in all the sights, sounds, and smells of that environment. The smell of alcohol, the sight of the doctors and nurses that I was totally dependent upon, even the sound of the ambulance pulling up with its siren reminded me that there was a massive need for the human race in the area of health and healing. The whole experience was the most humbling I had ever been through. I had not one ounce of pride left in me. Slammed to the floor and made to realize there is very little, if anything, I could control in this life, my mind went to a heightened sense of the purpose of my life! So, like Paul, I realized I needed to rely on my spiritual Father. When I came to this conclusion in my quiet moments at the hospital, I could feel a great surge of energy running through my body. This was especially true when I began to dream and visualize a future helping others.

Perhaps this was my purpose and the reason for my crisis: to encourage others, help others to find hope as I had, and to glorify my heavenly Father in the process. As these kinds of thoughts entered my mind, I became energized. I felt excited about my life, knowing I now had a very special mission.

My wife and I started listening to the CD together as my radiation therapy was scheduled.

I began asking questions, seeking answers.

"Ask and it will be given to you; seek and you will find; knock and the door will be opened to you."

Matthew 7:7 (NIV)

God opened my eyes to new possibilities—to hope.

He sent me other messages, this time by way of my wife. She was in turmoil. When you have sickness or adversity, all family members are affected. Sleepless and worried, she would wake in the middle of the night and turn on the TV. God reached out to her with messages from Dr. Wayne Dyer. His presentation moved her deeply, brought her comfort and hope. She ordered his book, *The Power of Intention*, and set of CDs. She knew Dyer's words and concepts were meant for me.

Wayne Dyer's message was foreign to me, and it took me some time to get my head around it. The more I listened and read, the more I knew he was talking about God and about how our thinking determines our world. Dyer wrote the book after a mild heart attack. He was inspired to write the book as he was waiting to have a surgical procedure to open a clogged artery. He knew what it meant to face a health crisis.

Words from the Wise

"When we change how we look at things, the things we look at change."

—Dr. Wayne Dyer, *The Power of Intention*

I was inspired to look at my life, my faith, and my healing process from a fresh perspective, with fresh intent.

I armed myself with tools of hope—positive ideas that brought me comfort, ahealing, and a fresh zest for life.

My wife was thrilled. She became a hunter-gatherer for fresh material and new insights from God. I thank the Lord for her love for Him and her love for me. Together we delved into the works of Tony Robbins, Joel Osteen, and the Bible in several translations, as I followed doctor's orders and started radiation treatments.

If we pay attention, God directs our path and provides answers.

Words from the Wise

"Thought is action in rehearsal."

—Sigmund Freud

"Beliefs have the power to create and the power to destroy."

—Tony Robbins

" . . . God will open doors for you and change circumstances on your behalf."

—Joel Osteen, *Your Best Life Now*

Joel Osteen was on TV one night talking about how to get through life when faced with adversity. Joel had a three-part series of awe-inspiring sermons. I ate them up. Joel's words helped me to understand I shouldn't try to control my situation in life, that I had God. He would handle it for me.

In case I had not gotten the message the first time, God sent me a minister who visited me in the hospital. I had never seen this man before. He had heard that I was sick through my son's Christian school. The verse he quoted to me reiterated what I had recently learned.

> "That is why, for Christ's sake, I delight in weakness, in insults, in hardships, in persecutions, in difficulties. **For when I am weak, then I am strong**."
>
> **2 Corinthians 12:10 (NIV)**

I had read that verse many times and never registered what it really meant. **When we connect to God and relinquish control, we become strong—through God's power.** This was an awakening, an epiphany. My eyes were opened. I started searching Scripture for answers and found them in droves. I had studied the Bible for fifty years and never fully comprehended the comfort to be found there until I needed it. I have believed in God since I was a small boy, but I never had the ultimate faith to live in His power. I thought He was locked away in Heaven and did not want to be bothered by little ole lowly me. I learned God longs to give us His everything. He is just waiting for us to invite Him into our lives.

I relinquished control and chose to walk with God.

Encouraging Scriptures

Come near to God and he will come near to you.

James 4:8 (NIV)

Seek good, not evil, that you may live. Then the **LORD God Almighty will be with you**, just as you say he is.

Amos 5:14 (NIV)

Obey me, and **I will be your God** and you will be my people. Walk in all the ways I command you, that **it may go well with you**.

Jeremiah 7:23 (NIV)

For the LORD gives wisdom, and from his mouth come knowledge and understanding. He holds victory in store for the upright, **he is a shield to those whose walk is blameless, for he guards the course** of the just and **protects the way** of his faithful ones.

Proverbs 2:6–8 (NIV)

Don't be afraid, I've redeemed you. I've called your name. **You're mine**. When you're in over your head, **I'll be there with you**. When you're in rough waters, **you will not go down**. When you're between a rock and a hard place, it won't be a dead end—**Because I am God, your personal God, The Holy of Israel, and your Savior**. I paid a huge price for you . . . that's how much you mean to me! **That's how much I love you**.

Isaiah 43:1–4 (MSG)

Steps I Used to Find Answers and Solutions

- I asked God why.
- I sought out and listened for His answers.
- I found comfort in new possibilities.
- I opened my eyes to hope.
- I found wisdom in the words of wise men.
- I embraced new concepts with fresh perspective.
- I started radiation treatments.
- I surrendered my crisis to God.
- I chose to walk nearer to God.

Three

Connecting to ***the*** Energy Source—God

When I began my cancer treatments, I started asking myself:

1. Can I control this situation?
2. What are my options?
3. How can I best get through treatment and heal from this cancer?
4. How can I tap into the healing energy sources within me?

I have to admit, I started out feeling like a victim. I had a radical surgical removal of my tonsils and all the lymph nodes on the left side of my neck. They found the cancer in my left tonsil. After recovering from my surgery, I visited my oncologist and prepared for additional treatments.

My oncologist predicted that:

1. My cancer would return in the first nine months.
2. The radiation would damage my throat so much that I would have to have a feeding tube placed in my stomach.
3. I would face forty long and painful radiation treatments.

He gave me the best option he had to offer for my type of cancer—radiation treatments—but no positive statements of hope that the cancer could be cured or thrown into remission.

I drew courage from a cancer survivor in my family. My mother had breast cancer when she was in her forties, which had metastasized to her lymph glands. She had a radical breast removal with radiation treatments. This was forty years ago. Cancer treatment was virtually in the Stone Age. When her doctors gave doom-filled prognoses she refused to accept them, but declared: "Don't tell me that I will not recover, because I know I will." She told the doctor, "I have four boys to take care of. I am going to live and not die!"

My mother, tenacious to say the least, is alive and well today. She served as an inspiration to me in my moment of darkness and gloom. I determined in my heart that this doctor did not know what my fate would be. The only being who knew my fate was God Almighty. I chose to take my doctor's treatments, but I chose not to believe in his gloomy predictions. Like my mother, I had a young son at home who needed me. I was going to live, not die!

I started each day off with a verse from the Bible that I made my own personal affirmation statement:

> "I can do all things through Christ who strengthens me."
>
> **Philippians 4:13 (NKJV)**

This uplifting statement of my faith brought me great confidence and positive energy. I could feel it boost my spirit and stamina.

I also meditated on a scripture that spoke to the hopeless place I was lifting myself out of and seemed to laugh in the face of despair:

"That is why, for Christ's sake, I delight in weaknesses, in insults, in hardships, in persecutions, in difficulties. **For when I am weak, then I am strong.**"

2 Corinthians 12:10 (NIV)

This scripture reminded me that it was okay to be weak, as long as I gave into the ultimate power source (God), because then I would be strong. When Christ was in His lowest, darkest moment—a moment of great pain, persecution, and the hardship of carrying His own cross—He demonstrated His greatest strength in willingly sacrificing himself for mankind. Out of His moment of greatest weakness, He demonstrated the glory of His ultimate power and strength.

Cancer was my moment of greatest weakness, and from it came the potential for my greatest strength. I felt that God had a plan for me to witness His glory and power as well as the strength and healing power within me. I felt like I needed to relinquish control and let Him lead me through this adversity. Surrendering to God and accessing His great energy gave me comfort. I didn't have anything to worry about. I felt deep in my soul that everything was going to be okay. God was in control. As I closed my eyes each evening to rest my weary body, I felt tremendous peace and comfort, knowing that God was going to take care of me and everything was going to be all right!

I was too tired to try to depend upon my own strength, which was all depleted. I had no solutions, no control, and no energy. I realized that God was my source, not the United States government, not Mom and Dad, not a company that paid my salary, not a doctor, not a minister, but the most powerful source of energy in this world and the next, GOD.

I had no other options except to trust in God's healing energy. I knew deep down that the radiation treatment was God's tool that was going to be part of his healing process. After the radiation treatments, God's loving energy would assist in my recovery from any damage the radiation did to healthy tissues.

I had felt that though I'd been given a death sentence, with God's help I could win reprieve. For me, this was my turning point in changing the course of my physical affliction. This all came together when I shifted my thought process to a higher standard of meditation and positive energy.

There will be no adversity that will win when God is on your side.

You may go through trials and tribulation, however, if you put your trust in the energy source—God—then the scriptures declare that no weapon shall prevail against you. Adversities will not win. You are promised protection from a divine source.

Words from the Wise

"A man's weakness and strength, purity and impurity, are his own and not another man's . . . they can only be altered by himself, never by another."

—James Allen

"Brains aren't designed to get results; they go in directions. If you know how the brain works you can set your own directions. If you don't, then someone else will."

—Richard Bandler

Healing Scriptures

Consider these scriptures that helped me so much during my time of despair:

Then your light will break forth like the dawn, and **your healing will quickly appear**; then your righteousness will go before you, and the glory of **the LORD will be your rear guard.**

Isaiah 58:8 (NIV)

"He who dwells in the shelter of the Most High will **rest in the shadow of the Almighty.** I will say of the **LORD, "He is my refuge and my fortress, my God, in whom I trust."**

Psalm 91:1–2 (NIV)

If anyone does attack you, it will not be my doing; whoever attacks you will surrender to you. "See, it is I who created the blacksmith who fans the coals into flame and forges a weapon fit for its work. And it is I who have created the destroyer to work havoc; **no weapon forged against you will prevail, and you will refute every tongue that accuses you. This is the heritage of the servants of the LORD, and this is their vindication from me," declares the LORD.**

Isaiah 54:15–17 (NIV)

Steps I Used to Heal My Body and My Mind

- I was inspired by a cancer survivor.
- I accepted my doctor's best treatment option, but I refused to believe his gloomy predictions for my survival.
- I started every day with a personal affirmation.
- I meditated on a scripture that laughed in the face of despair.
- I trusted in God to heal me.
- I shifted to a higher level of meditation.

Four

Where Could I Go But to the Lord—The Solution

I asked myself, *what is my solution?*

1. Who is in control?
2. Was I going to live?
3. How do I invoke God's involvement?
4. How can I build my body's immune system to assist in healing?
5. How can I relieve the stress in my life?
6. How can I obtain the feeling of well-being?

There is an old hymn entitled "Where Could I Go But to the Lord." This song is based on a conversation the Lord Jesus had with the Apostle Peter in John 6:68–69 (NIV). Jesus asked his remaining disciples if they wanted to leave him after some had left because they had no faith. Peter replied, "Lord, to whom shall we go? You have the words of eternal life. We believe and know that you are the Holy One of God." The apostle Peter sums up a very important answer to all our needs when it comes to all our problems and adversities, and that is: we have one and only one solution—Jesus Christ. Without Christ and His power I would not be living today.

"The Son [Jesus Christ] is the radiance of God's glory, and the exact representation of his being, **sustaining all things by his powerful word.** "

Hebrews 1:3 (NIV)

Christ indeed has the words of life. When I realized that all life flows through Him, I began to build my faith to the point of knowing. I used affirmations to help me reprogram my mind to think positive thoughts and to lean on the Lord for His healing.

I began to see and feel positive changes in my health when my thoughts were in harmony with the affirmation of the belief, faith, and knowledge that I would live and was under the protection of God. I went from thinking I was going to live to **KNOWING** I was going to live. There is a huge difference. I believe positive energy is created in my body when I think positively. When I think positive, happy, uplifting thoughts, I feel my energy increase. When I think negative doubt- and anxiety-filled thoughts, my energy levels sink. Try it. Think positively. I did. And I began to feel victory and joy in my heart, not the victim mentality that I had suffered at the beginning of my healing journey.

True change requires time. Stress or worry work hardship on the body's immune system. I chose to make several small but powerful positive changes in my life as a part of the process of healing. I chose to reduce the time I watched the news or listened to talk radio, both mainly negative information sources. I began to avoid friends and family who chose to have a negative outlook on life, and I surrounded myself with a support group of positive spirits.

I am also a big movie buff. I love to watch comedies and take myself out of my stressful world temporarily and into a fictitious world filled with laughter and lightheartedness. When you are ill, it can be healing to meditate, laugh, observe nature and animals, and even eat chocolate. These actions can stimulate the neurotransmitter serotonin in the brain, increasing the production of endorphins. Endorphins are released when we experience a sense of happiness, and this brain chemistry actually strengthens our immune system and can contribute to heart health, mental health, and faster healing. Endorphin/serotonin chemistry takes place in the opiate receptors of the brain. Like morphine, they can kill pain, give you a runner's sense of elation, or induce sleep. Some relieve feelings of depression while others are being linked to—surprise and good news!—the breaking down of cancer cells.

When the doctor gave me the diagnosis that I had stage IV squamous cell carcinoma, it was a bit like being hit upside the head with a two-by-four of doubt, fear, and negativity. The worst news of my life and an immediate loss of my sense of well-being came over me. This sinking, kick-in-the-gut feeling is the complete opposite of the feelings stimulated when I observe nature or watch a really funny, laugh-until-you-hurt movie. I consciously set out in search of that secure feeling, that I had taken for granted in the past, that "everything is okay."

In search of well-being, I found a great solace in meditating on the Fruits of the Spirit found in Galatians 5:22 (NIV): "But the fruit of the Spirit is love, joy, peace, patience, kindness, goodness, faithfulness."

When I thought and concentrated on these feelings and emotions, I once again was able to enlarge my energy capacity to another level. I felt good about my life and everything around me. Other examples of creating good feelings are when I touch someone I love, when I hold my wife's hand, or even when I love on my dog Sam. Sam would come and lie down by me when I would rest from my radiation treatments. I could feel his love, as if he somehow knew I was trying to heal and he wanted to help.

When I pet Sam I feel warmth and affection coming from him. It brings me to tears sometimes. Dogs never ask any questions, never reject your love, never say negative words to hurt your feelings—they only want to be near you and love on you. Sam does like to play, eat, and go for a walk, but other than that he demands nothing from me. I advise anyone needing to heal to get a dog. Dogs have been shown to assist in the healing process, especially with children and the elderly.

I took advice from 1 Corinthians 13:3 (NIV) which says: "If I give all I possess to the poor and surrender my body to the flames, **but have not love, I gain nothing.**" Love will send a stronger frequency for healing than any other emotion you can have. Use love as a positive force to assist in the healing process.

I also find happiness, enthusiasm, soothing calm, and peacefulness in certain pieces of music. During my recovery time, I listened to music for hours. My energy level was not very good for four to six weeks after my radiation treatments had ended, and so I would lay in my recliner, with Sam at my feet, and listen to soothing music. I had a band in Dallas for almost ten years and have loved music since I was a small child, so it proved very therapeutic to me.

Science backs me up. I have learned that music has been lab tested on the growth rate of plants for years and that vintners in Italy use music to help grow stronger grape vines. "Music has been shown to help reduce post-surgical stress and pain, to reduce symptoms of depression in home-bound elderly people, and to aid children who are developmentally delayed by enhancing hand-eye coordination" (Wicke 2002). That sounds like a potentially healing thing to me. What I know for certain is that music relaxed me and put me in a calmer, happier, more peaceful state of mind. All of which assist my body and my mind throughout the process of healing.

In the Bible we are told that David played his harp to lift King Saul's spirit.

> "Whenever the spirit from God came upon Saul, David would take his harp and play. Then relief would come to Saul; he would feel better, and the evil spirit would leave him."
>
> **1 Samuel 16:23 (NIV)**

Holistic healers are developing a whole new healing practice based on sound and the power of the human voice. Healing through happiness, laughter, music, and uplifting voices—I loved those ideas, especially since they involved something I had control over. I could choose to be happy, even though my circumstances were not happy ones. I could choose to be a positive spirit in this, the most negative moment of my life. So, I walked with Sam by Lake Ray Hubbard, which borders our backyard, meditated daily on God's beauty in nature, listened to music and Dr. Wayne Dyer's soothing meditation CD, and started writing a healing book which contained all my favorite scriptures. I meditated on these scriptures daily and learned about the power of prayer and affirmations.

Words from the Wise

"I think music in itself is healing. It's an explosive expression of humanity. It's something we are all touched by. No matter what culture we're from, everyone loves music."

—Billy Joel

"It's part of the calling to at least do a few songs in the show that give people some hope . . . music is such a great healing balm."

—Ricky Skaggs

Prayer

The Healing Power of a Talk with God

Prayer is simply our communication with God. We can pray in petition to God, in praise to God, or in thanksgiving to God. Jesus said, "Until now you have not asked for anything in my name. Ask and you will receive, and your joy will be complete," (John 16:24 NIV). Prayer gives God access to your life and allows Him to work to deliver your requests.

I end any prayer with "In Jesus Christ's name, I pray." Also, when I pray in a petition-type prayer, I ask only once for each request. **I believe that God answers my prayers.** If I keep on asking and asking, does that demonstrate faith in Him? The answer to your prayers may take time, so stay strong in faith. Christ's sacrifice on the cross has put us back in God's good graces. Christ is now our High Priest who makes us priests in service to God.

Thank the Lord Jesus for His most wonderful gifts.

"Unlike the other high priests, he does not need to offer sacrifices day after day, first for his own sins, and then for the sins of the people. He sacrificed for their sins once for all when he offered himself."

Hebrews 7:27 (NIV)

"To him who loves us and has freed us from our sins by his blood, and has made us to be a kingdom and priests to serve his God and Father—to him be glory and power for ever and ever! Amen."

Revelation 1:6 (NIV)

"I write these things to you who believe in the name of the Son of God so that you may know you have eternal life. This is the confidence that we have in approaching God: that **if we ask anything according to his will, he hears us.** And if we know that he hears us—whatever we ask—we know that **we have what we asked of him.**"

1 John 5:13–15 (NIV)

Be confident that He hears us. We then know that He will give us what we ask for. This simply means that we know **God is our God.** He listens and gives us our requests. This is simply faith. Faith that **knows** beyond a shadow of a doubt that God can and will give us what we ask for. I knew I needed to be living and walking with God (obeying his commands) and doing what pleases Him. As I have stated before, I reconciled myself to God. I wanted Him on my side. I worked hard at following His will, which means doing what the New Testament has instructed us to do.

What gave me even more security, was the knowledge that we even have access to the Holy Spirit who assists us when we are too weary to pray or to confused to know what to ask. At times I was so weary that I really didn't know just what to pray for. In times like these, the Holy Spirit steps in and conveys our message to God. This comforted me, knowing I had spiritual assistance in my time of need.

I also noticed that I needed to be asking for things that were pleasing to Him. When I read the Bible, I am learning God's will. In the past, I have actually believed that somehow God's will was changing. It is not!

I know God's will from the Old and New Testaments. God's Word is just like a will that is left for the children of a deceased person. The will spells out exactly what is expected of the heir to rightly inherit what the will has stipulated. If a testator, one who has made a testament or will, states in a will that the recipient has to live in the inherited house in order to get the house, then anything other than that action will break the will. The same thing goes for me. If I am not living by God's will and testament, as revealed in the New Testament, then He is not obligated to give me my desires. If I am walking with God and He is walking with me, then I can boldly go before His throne and ask Him directly for my healing or anything else I need. Of course, I believe that I live everyday only because God has granted it to me.

From 2000 until 2007, the United States government spent $2.3 million on grants to study the power of prayers. In every study that I found, there were no tests of prayers by sick individuals praying for themselves. Every study was someone else praying for the sick, not the sick person praying for him or herself. These studies of prayer for others showed little results for the power of prayer. In one study, however, there was an 11 percent reduction in the illnesses or effects of heart disease for the study group.

Powerful Scriptures

Dear friends, if our hearts do not condemn us, we have confidence before God and **receive from him anything we ask**, because we obey his commands and do what pleases him.

1 John 3:21–22 (NIV)

In the same way, the **Spirit helps us in our weakness.** We do not know what we ought to pray for, but the Spirit himself intercedes for us with groans that words cannot express.

Romans 8:26 (NIV)

Therefore do not be foolish, but understand what the Lord's will is.

Ephesians 5:17 (NIV)
(This verse declares that God has a will and it can be understood.)

Therefore, since we have a great high priest who has gone through the heavens, Jesus the Son of God, let us hold firmly to the faith we profess. For we do not have a high priest who is unable to sympathize with our weaknesses, but we have one who has been tempted in every way, just as we are—yet was without sin. Let us then **approach the throne of grace with confidence,** so that we may receive mercy and **find grace to help us in our time of need.**

Hebrews 4:14–16 (NIV)

I believe that prayers from family and friends can bring you positive energy and a feeling of emotional support, but true healing must come from within. I believe that the sinner must pray for forgiveness of his own sins. I believe the ill must pray for their healing. This was the hardest thing for me to understand. I had spent my life in church praying for the sick. I believe the Bible supports our praying for the sick, but the individual that is sick holds the key to his own healing. I believe that healing must be invoked by the person that is sick through his faith, mind, and prayers. Through my faith, I believed I could be healed by the power of God within me. Through your faith, do you believe you can be healed by the power of God within? I encourage you to pray for your own healing.

Affirmations

Affirmations are simply a statement of faith. With affirmations we can instill in our mind and body a positive thought, premise, or idea. Affirmations give the mind and body permission to access the entire potential God gave us.

One of my many problems during my illness was to get my mind going down the correct path. I knew that if I was going to be successful in my healing, I would have to possess great faith. I knew I needed the kind of faith that has no doubts in the outcome. I had always been the type of person that felt I either didn't deserve God's favor or didn't think He used His powers on us today. I found all this to be false. I studied the scriptures and found numerous accounts of where God is longing to help His children.

I searched for ways to help me reprogram my negative beliefs. I found that affirmations help in getting the mind to change its beliefs. I wanted to plant in my mind positive truths that come from God's word to help me see the healing vision.

The key to affirmations is repetition. Recite them aloud to yourself repeatedly or write them down repeatedly. The idea is repeat, repeat, repeat throughout the day to reprogram your subconscious mind. When the subconscious accepts these thoughts as reality, the conscious mind, body, and spirit seek to meet that inner expectation and can ultimately manifest change. You create your own reality by how you think.

"For as he thinks within himself, so he is."

Proverbs 23:7 (NASB)

Reprogramming negative thinking to a positive outlook takes time. You cannot do this process for a day and think that you have erased years of internal criticism. You become what you think and say, so don't underestimate the power you possess in such words and ideas. Words and thoughts send messages from your brain, programming what comes next in your body, in your actions, and in your healing process.

Neuro-Linguistic Programming (NLP) is the psychoanalytical practice behind understanding the relationship between verbal stimuli to the brain and the resulting behavioral patterns. Think of your mind as your computer. What you program into your mental computer establishes a pattern for how your psyche will react given certain stimuli. Combined with faith, prayer, and hope, NLP is a very powerful tool that can increase an individual's understanding of how words have affected who we are.

Hope and faith are among our greatest assets and are one of the main reasons why placebos (sugar pills used in clinical studies) have a great track record in healing. If your mind tells your body that it should perform a certain way, it usually does. We also know how effective prayer can be for an individual when it is combined with faith and hope. When a person feels doomed in the face of a disease such as cancer, the body may just quit trying. As a patient, I could see that I had great powers with the potential to work for, or against, the healing process within me.

I believed my body's natural healing power could be harnessed to heal itself. The statement of such a powerful, positive, uplifting belief is called an affirmation. I started each day with meditation and my affirmation statements. Here are powerful affirmations you can use to reprogram your mind and spirit. It is important that the words feel comfortable to you and are in-line with who you are. If these are not suitable, write affirmations that fit your beliefs or situation and repeat them each day in a meditative state.

I would get up every morning and say out loud with conviction:

1. I am healed and am completely healthy in all ways.
2. My body is perfect as God has made it.
3. I'm getting better and better every day in every way.
4. I am filled with the light and energy of God.
5. "With God all things are possible." —Matthew 19:26 (NIV)
6. I am perfectly healthy in body, mind, and spirit.
7. I can do all things in Christ Jesus to become completely well.
8. I am healthy and free of all disease.
9. I am healthy, happy, and at peace with God.
10. I possess all of God's power to heal my body.
11. I have all the energy God has given me to fulfill my healing needs.
12. God's love heals me and makes me whole.
13. My body is healed, restored, and filled with God's energy.
14. I am healthy.

I tell myself regularly that I am a healthy, vibrant person, made in the image of God. I state it over and over until I know it is true. Live from the belief that you no longer are sick, that you have been completely healed and have vibrant health. Above all, say constantly: "Thank you Lord for my healing!"

Words from the Wise

Your prayer is a switch, allowing the power of God to flow into your life and through you."

—Frederick K. C. Price, *Answered Prayer Guaranteed*

"[Affirmations] have been shown to promote regeneration and rejuvenation of the body."

—Jeff Staniforth, "How Do Affirmations Promote Vibrant Health and Well-Being?"

Healing Scriptures

Through faith you are kept safe by God's power.

1 PETER 1:5 (NIRV)

But the Lord is faithful, and he will
strengthen and protect you.

2 Thessalonians 3:3 (NIV)

And the power of the Lord was present
for him to **heal the sick.**

Luke 5:17 (NIV)

Pray for each other so **that you may be healed.**
The prayer of a righteous man is powerful and effective.

James 5:16 (NIV)

Steps I Used to Heal My Body and My Mind

- I surrendered to God.
- I asked God for His healing through prayer.
- I believed God had answered my prayer—I had faith.
- I lived in the belief that I had been healed.
- I was thankful each day.
- I increased my energy with a positive outlook.
- I chose positive activities and voices over negative.
- I stopped watching the news.
- I listened to soothing music.
- I watched funny movies.
- I enjoyed the beauty of nature, the healing energy of loved ones, and my pet.
- I meditated on positive daily affirmations of health and healing.
- I stated my beliefs aloud daily.

Five

God's Power—Is He with Us Today?

I questioned my belief system:

1. Has God abandoned me in this world?
2. How do I access God's power?
3. Is God up in heaven or in a box?
4. Is God's power limited?
5. Can I limit my power?

During my stroke and then the cancer, my belief system was tested to the max. My wife Mary Beth and I needed God more than any time in our previous years. We were both raised as Christians in very conservative churches. As I grew up, I developed a belief system that did not rely on God for my everyday existence. My belief system had God up in heaven, isolated from His children, and our only access to Him was through His Word. In order for me to access God's healing powers, I had to develop my belief system through studying the scriptures and enlarging my vision. I changed my vision from one of no expectation from God to unlimited expectation from the God that controls the universe.

God can and will do anything I ask, according to His will, based upon my faith.

"This is the confidence we have in approaching God: that if we ask **anything according to his will**, he hears us. And if we know that he hears us—**whatever we ask—we know that we have what we asked of him.**"

1 John 5:14–15 (NIV)

I once believed that God wasn't interested in our problems and that we shouldn't bother Him through prayer; if we got sick with a disease, it would be better if we just died. Of course the Word of God says the exact opposite. It is a sad day when a person thinks the only option available to him is to be a victim of circumstance in a world with no solutions. I beg to differ.

There is a solution, and the reason I know this is because God's Word tells me so. I started searching the scriptures for how God deals with us today. What I found was that God is just waiting to help his children and give them favor and miracles. God is everywhere, seeking out those who are thinking His thoughts and is just waiting to bless them with all He has.

"So that your faith might not rest on men's wisdom, but on God's **power.** "

1 Corinthians 2:5 (NIV)

I was speaking to a fellow Christian the other day who was so downtrodden and depressed. We began talking about the power of prayer, and she said that she had almost gotten to the point of "Why even pray?" If you ever get to this point in your life when you think or question the ability to pray and get positive answers, then you really and truly have no hope left.

Has God abandoned us today? Is God up in Heaven or locked up or in a box? Can I count on God to answer my prayers for my physical concerns as well as my spiritual needs?

Unfortunately, there is a vast sect of people in the religious community that for one reason or another believe that God does not work directly in a personal relationship today with His children. In other words, God will not use His power on us directly but only through the natural, physical elements of this world. In this case, we can no longer use words like "miracle."

The only thing that limits God is our weak-thinking of His power or our lack of faith!
Do not limit the Holy One—He lives on streets of gold!

When we reference the Old Testament, it is for the purposes of obtaining greater hope and knowing God.

> "Everything that was written in the past was written to teach us, so that through endurance and encouragement of the scriptures we might have **hope.**"
>
> **Romans 15:4 (NIV)**

That is what this book is all about: **hope.** Without hope, we have nothing. This is a lesson I learned the hard way, going through rehab after my stroke and through two surgeries and radiation therapy for my cancer. So remember, when I reference a scripture from the Old Testament, don't discard it, but rather embrace it in the name of Hope.

Words from the Wise

"There is no medicine like hope, no incentive so great, and no tonic so powerful as expectation of something tomorrow."

—Orison Swett Marden

"Most of the important things in the world have been accomplished by people who have kept on trying when there seemed to be no hope at all."

—Dale Carnegie

Scriptures of Hope

May the God **of hope** fill you with all joy and peace as **you trust in him,** so that you may overflow with **hope by the power** of the Holy Spirit.

Romans 15:13 (NIV)

Guide me in your truth and teach me, for you are God my Savior, and **my hope** is in you all day long.

Psalm 25:5 (NIV)

We wait in **hope** for the LORD; he is our help and our shield.

Psalm 33:20 (NIV)

They turned back and tempted God **and limited the Holy One of Israel.**

Psalm 78:41 (KJV)

They **did not believe in God** or trust in his deliverance.

Psalm 78:22 (NIV)

Jesus Christ is the same yesterday and today and forever.

Hebrews 13:8 (NIV)

Therefore I tell you, do not worry about your life, what you will eat or drink....Look at the birds of the air; they do not sow or reap or store away in barns, and **yet your heavenly Father feeds them.**

Matthew 6:25–26 (NIV)

When we lose our faith or when our faith is weakened, we start putting limits on God. If we never learn to totally trust in God's power, then we cannot learn to walk in the Spirit with God or expect our lives to change for the better. Another factor to consider is that God has not changed. God still loves His children just like He did in Old Testament times. God may use different techniques and tools to help us today, but God can and does work on us directly today, using His power to heal us and give us favor.

In Numbers 11:23 (NASB) God asked Moses, "Is the LORD'S power limited?" This same question beckons us today to reflect inside our hearts and ask: "Has God left me?" "Can I no longer depend upon God for anything in this physical world?" "Has He lost His power?" Let us answer that with some scripture:

Power of God

"The weapons we fight with are not the weapons of the world. On the contrary, they have divine **power** to demolish strongholds."

2 Corinthians 10:4 (NIV)

"Summon your **power,** O God; show us your strength, O God, as you have done before."

Psalm 68:28 (NIV)

Do not be afraid to ask God for favor. If we are His child, it is our inherited right! He wants to help you!

How Does God's Power Protect Us?

We know that anyone born of God does not continue to sin; the one who was born of God keeps him safe, and the **evil one cannot harm him.**

1 John 5:18 (NIV)

"My prayer is not that you take them out of the world but that you **protect them from the evil one.**"

John 17:15 (NIV)

Steps I Used to Invoke God's Power

- I put my hope in God.
- I believed without doubts that God was with me.
- I trusted in God.
- I did not limit God.
- I believed in God's power.
- I believed that God walked with me.
- I believed God can and will use His powers to help me.

Six

Healing through Faith

I questioned my faith:

1. Is my healing affected by my faith?
2. What has faith got to do with answered prayers?
3. How do I keep my faith in the midst of this chaos?
4. How do I build my faith to the point of no doubting?
5. Can someone else ask God to heal me?

To advance my healing state, I realized that I had to build my faith in God in order for my healing to be complete. In every verse that I could find in the Bible that speaks of healing or praying for healing, is declared: "**let it be done according to your faith.**" So my healing had to be centered on my faith in God and that He would answer my prayers. The kind of trust that God wants from us, is exactly like that which Joshua and Caleb demonstrated when they were ready to go to battle with the giants in the land of Canaan. Simply put, they knew they had a mighty God on their side, and thus all things were possible. They did not doubt God's involvement in their battles or His power to accomplish anything.

What Is Faith?

It is the ability to know without question, to have no doubts. Examine this analogy:

Do you have a brain? Have you seen, touched, smelled, heard, or tasted your brain? Then how do you know you have a brain? Simply because you see the results, because without a brain, how could you sustain life? Therefore, you know you have a brain. No doubts.

This is the same way you must have faith in God. You know absolutely that this world, as magnificent as it is, could not be created without a creator. So your faith is built block by block through your experiences and education in this world. Then your faith starts to build on other people's testimonies. I believe that Jesus Christ came to earth as a man and sacrificed His life so that I might be justified by his blood. I didn't see Christ die on the cross, but through the testimonies of witnesses, I believe that He did die on the cross. And what is more important is that He rose from the dead. He did something we cannot do for ourselves.

Words from the Wise

"Faith is reason plus revelation, and the revelation
part requires one to think with the spirit
as well as with the mind . . . hear the music,
not just read the notes."

—Francis S. Collins, M.D., Ph.D.

"If you think you can, or if you think you cannot,
both are correct."

—Henry Ford

"I cannot always control what goes on outside, but
I can control what goes on inside,"

—Dr. Wayne Dyer

Again, block by block, I built my faith. I read God's Word which, together with life's experiences, would build my faith.

For example, I know that God saved my life when I had my stroke.

Seeking Him is also a very powerful process. If we seek God and His path for us, then He will show it to us. Some people believe that we cannot ask for anything physical. God wants us to ask Him to walk with us here on earth.

I believe the hardest thing I had to do in my entire healing process was to keep my faith. My faith was constantly being tested from the medical world, which legally cannot give you much hope in cancer recovery, to my family and church members telling me that it would be better for me to just die and go to heaven. I wasn't ready to leave this life. I had things to do and a young child to raise and love. So many times I fought the feelings of doubt.

I began to think of my connection to God as a power line carrying electricity or, in my case, energy. This power line is of no value if it loses connectivity from the power source (God). I pictured my faith as the security device holding my power line connection to God. If ever broken, then my energy source was severed. I had to stay connected through my faith.

Once I found all the Bible verses below, I put them into my

healing book. I would read them at the beginning of each day when I would begin my meditation exercise. These verses reaffirmed my faith, and each day my faith grew. These verses are powerful because they showed me that if I had faith, and did not doubt that God would be involved in my life, then God would give me His healing power.

Faith Scriptures

And without **faith** it is impossible to please God, because anyone who comes to him must believe that he exists and that **he rewards** those who earnestly seek him.

Hebrews 11:6 (NIV)

I pray that out of his glorious riches he may strengthen you **with power through his Spirit in your inner being**, so that Christ may dwell in your hearts through **faith.**

Ephesians 3:16–17 (NIV)

But when he asks, he must **believe and not doubt**, because he who doubts is like a wave of the sea, blown and tossed by the wind. That man should not think he will receive anything from the Lord; he is a double-minded man, unstable in all he does.

James 1:6–8 (NIV)

For this reason I kneel before the Father, from whom his whole family in heaven and on earth derives its name. I pray that out of his glorious riches he may strengthen you **with power through his Spirit in your inner being,** so that Christ may dwell in your hearts through faith. And I pray that you, being rooted and established in love, may have **power**, together with all the saints, to grasp how wide and long and high and deep is the **love of Christ**, and **to know this love that surpasses knowledge**—that you may be filled to the measure of all the fullness of God. Now to him who is able to **do immeasurably more than all we ask or imagine, according to his power that is at work within us**, to him be glory in the church and in Christ Jesus throughout all generations, for ever and ever! Amen.

Ephesians 3:14–21 (NIV)

Jesus replied, "I tell you the truth, if **you have faith and do not doubt**, not only can you do what was done to the fig tree, but also you can say to this mountain, 'Go, throw yourself into the sea,' and it will be done."

Matthew 21:21 (NIV)

What is this power that is at work within us? It is our mind and spirit. The mind is very, very powerful, and when it is backed by faith in God, it is limitless!

Healing Scriptures of Faith

And a woman was there who had been subject to bleeding for twelve years, but no one could heal her. She came up behind him and touched the edge of his cloak, and immediately her bleeding stopped.

"Who touched me?" Jesus asked.

When they all denied it, Peter said, "Master, the people are crowding and pressing against you."

But Jesus said, "Someone touched me; I know that power has gone out from me."

Then the woman, seeing that she could not go unnoticed, came trembling and fell at his feet. In the presence of all the people, she told why she had touched him and how she had been instantly healed.

Then he said to her, "Daughter, your faith has healed you. Go in peace."

Luke 8:43–48 (NIV)

> Then Jesus said to the centurion, "Go! It will be done just as you believed it would."
>
> **Matthew 8:13 (NIV)**

Now there is one thing God does not tell us, and that is *when* He will answer our prayers. He answers our prayers when it is the perfect time, and not one second sooner. I kept telling myself that God was at work in my life and that all things would come together in His perfect timing.

So **by faith, I had to pray and visualize the prayer as being fulfilled** and it was so. I never lost site of the answered prayer—the end result. I never **doubted**, and I **never gave up.** God had done His part to give me His peace. As a child of God, His peace is on the inside of me right now. I've got to do my part and trust God.

Keep the faith!

In almost all of Christ's healings a measure of faith was required. Christ did not heal anyone against his or her will.

"And he did not do many miracles there
because of their lack of faith."

Matthew 13:58 (NIV)

For the person that is being healed, faith is absolutely the key to all healings.

The question is then: Can someone else ask God to heal me?

I believe the request and faith must come from the person that is sick. God cannot enter our lives if we do not ask Him to. That would violate our free will. Once I have asked God for His healing powers, the only thing holding God back is my faith. I am the one controlling the throttle, so to speak. If I let God into my life to walk with me, He will do exactly what He has said in His Word.

Faith is the key to all prayers.

If we are walking with God and He is walking with us, then we can boldly go before His throne and ask Him directly for our healing.

You will also notice that we have to be asking for things that are pleasing to Him or that are not against His will. If we ask for something of an evil nature, you can be assured God will not answer it in the affirmative. In fact, this negative energy will bring bad things back to the requester. However, if we are asking for our healing, there is no place in the Bible that gives us any direct guidance that those requests would be against His will. Therefore, we should have confidence that His will is to give us healing.

"You want something but don't get it. You kill and covet, but you cannot have what you want. You quarrel and fight. **You do not have, because you do not ask God.**"

James 4:2 (NIV)

As long as our motives are pure when we ask for things, and if we are following God's will, **we have not simply because we ask not.** I believe God wants us to ask for all our needs so that He can help us and walk with us in our lives here on earth. We are His children and He loves us!

I believe God speaks to us about faith, because faith is simply getting our minds to accept something unseen.

Steps I Used to Build My Faith

- I read powerful scriptures on faith each day.
- I believed, without doubts, that God was with me.
- I searched God's Word for answers.
- I did not limit God.
- I asked God for His healing.
- I made sure I was asking according to His will.
- I tried to think like God.
- I depended on God and leaned on His wonderful powers.

Seven

Healing through Visualization—God's Vision for Me

I began searching for anything to assist in my healing:

1. How does the mental practice of visualizations help in my healing?
2. How can I build up my faith and my hope?
3. How can I engage my mind to be part of my healing?
4. What exactly is meditation, and how can it assist me in healing?

During my radiation treatment, the doctors and nurses who were ministering to me expected that I would be forced to have a feeding tube put into my stomach. Almost all patients with my cancer and treatment would be so burned in the mouth and throat that they would not be able to swallow or eat. Some could not even handle swallowing their own saliva.

I held close a different vision for myself throughout my forty radiation treatments.

I put my faith in God, that He would heal me and that I would never have cancer again. I told myself each day that I came from a very big God and was made perfectly in His image. I meditated on God and His power. I had no doubts. I went through a mental visualization of breathing in healthy, vibrant cells and exhaling the sick and weak cells.

I visualized myself in my most perfect body, when I was around twenty-five. I was lean and muscular. I had great energy and could run miles and never get fatigued. I pictured my spirit as perfection, God's perfect creation of me. I pictured God's energy coming into my body and repairing my physical body to reflect my spiritual body. I pictured my healed body radiating with vibrant energy.

I knew beyond a shadow of a doubt that God was healing me.

I never had the horrible problems the doctors and nurses envisioned for me. I did reach a point where I didn't want real food because the radiation treatments affected my salivary glands, which determine your sense of taste. Food tasted awful. I lived on protein drinks. I lost fifty pounds, but it took only two months after I finished the treatments to get my taste back and to eat real food. The doctors were amazed that I went through so many radiation treatments and came out with no permanent adverse effects.

If you have prayed to be healed of cancer, you must know deep down in your heart, your soul, your fingers and toes, that God is healing you. This is where affirmation and visualization come into view. Using these tools helped my subconscious mind to accept this and act upon the idea. If I doubted that God had healed me, then He had not. Faith is the key!

God works through men of medicine. They assist Him in treating disease.

However:

Do not allow negative statements or dire prognostications concerning your future to become your belief system.

The mind is the control point of body and spirit. What the mind takes in usually stays there. So if someone tells you that you cannot do some task when you are five years old, you will still remember that you cannot do that task at fifty. As with a computer: Garbage in, Garbage out. However, just like a computer, you can reprogram your mind to delete those negative remarks and download new, positive remarks. This takes time, but it is relatively simple to do.

> "Oh yes, you shaped me first inside, then out; you formed me in my mother's womb. I thank you, High God—you're breathtaking! Body and soul, I am marvelously made! I worship in adoration—what a creation! You know me inside and out, you know every bone in my body; you know exactly how I was made, bit by bit, how I was sculpted from nothing into something. Like an open book, you watched me grow from conception to birth; all the stages of my life were spread out before you, the days of my life all prepared before I'd even lived one day."
>
> **Psalm 139:13–16 (MSG)**

This is God's vision for each of us.

Visualizations

We all have heard the old Chinese proverb which states: "One picture is worth ten thousand words." That really is what visualization is all about. Visualization is a tool anyone can use to assist them in a healing process, in perfecting a sporting task, for taking fear out of our minds, for being a successful business person, or any other thing you are working on to better yourself physically, mentally, or spiritually. By providing positive pictures in the form of creative imagery and self-suggestion, visualization can change body chemistry which subsequently has a physical effect on our bodies. For instance, if we are watching a scary movie, our bodies can actually produce adrenaline to assist in protecting itself, thus changing our body chemistry.

If we see it, we can be it.

When I went through radiation therapy for cancer in my left tonsil, they built a plastic mask for my head that covered down to my mid chest. They would then lock that mask down on the table where I lay. This would enable them to move the lasers of radiation to a specific spot without the fear that they would sever my spine. Well that sounds great in theory, but when they would bolt that mask down to the table my mind would become frantic with fear—fear that I couldn't breathe or move. It was an absolutely terrifying experience. I just didn't think I could lie there for an hour each day for forty days.

My doctor prescribed some drug that would relax me and enable me to go on with the treatments. I took the drug and went in for the first real treatment. I felt so relaxed and was sure that I could endure the mask. Well when they bolted that mask down on the table, my adrenaline went into overdrive, and I begged to be released. I tried this for several days and each time my adrenaline would outwork the drugs, no matter how much they gave me. The solution was to trim the mask back to cover only my face and reduce the treatment time to fifteen minutes. I decided after a week of using the relaxing drug, which would make me sleep for hours after each treatment and made me feel terrible each day, that I could somehow teach my mind to endure the mask.

So I stopped taking the relaxation drug and instead took my mind on a trip to places that I loved. The places I visualized were Lake Tahoe; Cannon Beach, Oregon; and Hawaii. You see, I love vacations in beautiful places where I feel as though I can witness the fingerprints of God.

I not only visualized these beautiful sites in my mind, but I could also feel the physical elements of their substance. For example, I remembered Cannon Beach, Oregon, as a place where I could smell the ocean, feel the cool air against my skin, and see prism colors in sunlit ocean spray against the rocks. With visualizations like this, I got through radiation therapy without drugs.

Visualize what makes you come alive with passion for God's beauty. Your brain is a very powerful God-given tool. Do not waste it! Put it to use.

Developing and Using the Visualization Tool:

I learned a lot about brains when I had my stroke, really more than I wanted to learn. I had a right brain bleed which paralyzed my left side. I had to learn to walk and use my left arm again. I had to relearn how to type with both hands. To this day, when I sit down at a computer I only want to use my right hand. I have to consciously bring my left hand to the computer.

I do not really have any other side effects except that I am more emotional than I ever was—I can cry at the drop of a hat—but I've also learned that anyone can add functionality to the brain that it didn't have before.

There have been studies that claim we only use a portion of our mind's potential, some state usage is as low as 10 percent. When I was in rehab after my stroke, there was a young man of twenty-one there who had a stroke while performing a physical (PT) test for the army. His brain was bleeding, and he had to have surgery to stop it. The doctors had to take out almost half of his brain. Of course that left him unable to walk or do simple tasks; however, after many months of rehab he was able to carry on a fairly normal life. He reprogrammed the other half to do the functions that had been previously performed by the side of the brain that was taken out. If we can have 50 percent of our brain removed and still carry on a normal life, just think what we might be able to do if we used that extra 50 percent completely.

When I had the stroke it literally killed sections of my brain. Therefore, the part of the brain that once told me that I had a left arm no longer worked. Rehabilitation was imperative. The therapists taught me how to reprogram my brain to develop those lost functions in a part of the brain that was not being used. I have been told that only 10 percent of people that have strokes regain complete functionality. The only way you can tell that I have had a stroke—which completely paralyzed my left side—is that when I smile, my mouth droops just a little. I think this is miraculous. My feeling is that if anyone can add new functions to their brains why should other healing not also be possible?

There is a theory that says the right side of the brain is where creativity resides. The left side of the brain is where logic and the ability to use words and reasoning resides. The right brain is very important in implementing the visualization tool that I used to keep my mind centered on healing. The right brain also knows no logic and can guide me to my goals without judgment or reason. So if I believe in my mind that I am healed, then my right brain is the part that will make it happen. If you are a left-brain dominant person (mathematicians, doctors, etc.), then you may have more challenges in the visualization and healing process. Left-brain dominant thinkers are not as adept at using the creative side of their brains; however, they can develop the right brain to assist in the healing process. Visualization is really a good tool to accomplish this. The right brain asks no questions, it just performs required functions. So when I visualize a healthy body, the right brain participates without conflict.

Visualization through Meditation:

I believe this tool really boosted the healing process in my body and programmed positive images into my mind that I still carry day to day, improving my immune system and producing healing chemicals in my body. I started out meditating for three minutes and built up to thirty minutes. The more my mind interacts with my body, the more I believe healing takes place.

In deep meditation, brain activity is characterized by theta waves, which demonstrate a connection to our subconscious mind. There is active research examining the healing properties of theta and delta brain-wave activity. It is believed that in these deep- or near-sleep stages of brain activity, healing takes place.

1. Start by quieting your mind. Get in an isolated room and close out the world. You can use soothing music or just quietness, whatever is best for you. Begin to relax your body, starting with your head, and feel the muscles begin to relax, going all the way to your toes.
2. Breathe deeply and then exhale slowly and completely.
3. Feel God's energy come into your body. I picture a ball of swirling energy coming into my head and then passing

throughout my body, healing all parts as it goes from head to toe.

4. Picture yourself in the most perfect healthy condition, in the most beautiful place you can imagine. I would picture myself healthy and fit in my favorite places like on a beach in Hawaii or Carmel, California.

Remember your mind and spirit are telling your body how it feels, how it appears, and how it heals. I remind my body that it is a reflection of my most perfect spirit. I tell myself that my body was built with DNA from God, and that the cells within me have the power to heal. And I would repeat this verse that I had memorized:

> "I pray also that the eyes of your heart may be enlightened in order that you may know . . . his incomparably **great power for us who believe.** That power is like the working of his mighty strength."
>
> **Ephesians 1:18–19 (NIV)**

Healing Scriptures

According to your faith will it be done to you.

Matthew 9:29 (NIV)

But those who hope in the LORD will renew their strength. They will soar on wings like eagles; they will run and not grow weary, they will walk and not be faint.

Isaiah 40:31 (NIV)

"You don't have enough faith," Jesus told them. "I tell you the truth, **if you had faith even as small as a mustard seed**, you could say to this mountain, 'Move from here to there,' and it would move. **Nothing would be impossible**."

Matthew 17:20 (NLT)

"Have faith in God," Jesus answered. "I tell you the truth, if anyone says to this mountain, 'Go, throw yourself into the sea,' and does not doubt in his heart but believes that what he says will happen, it will be done for him. Therefore I tell you, **whatever you ask for in prayer, believe that you have received it, and it will be yours."**

Mark 11:22–24 (NIV)

Words from the Wise

"Only those who can see the invisible can accomplish the impossible."

—Patrick Snow, *Creating Your Own Destiny*

"The potential of the human mind is subject to, and limited only by, our individual beliefs or un-belief as to whether we can accomplish a thing or not."

—Chuck Danes

"Formulate and stamp indelibly on your mind a mental picture of yourself as succeeding. Hold this picture tenaciously. Never permit it to fade. Your mind will seek to develop this picture."

—Norman Vincent Peale

"The effectiveness of suggestion has been demonstrated over and over again in every field of medicine and human behavior . . . in practically every instance of research on drugs with humans, suggestion has been proven effective."

—Dr. Charles Henderson, PhD, *Self Hypnosis for the Life You Want*

Steps I Used to Heal through Visualization

- I held a healthy vision of my body.
- I put my faith in God, that He would heal me.
- I visualized myself in my most perfect body.
- I reprogrammed my mind to think positive thoughts.
- I used visualization to make it through radiation treatments.
- I meditated daily.
- I visually felt God's healing energy entering my body to heal me.
- I pictured my cancer being eliminated by my immune system.

Believing You Are Healed

I searched for answers from God:

1. What tools has God given us to heal our bodies?
2. Is my body a reflection of what I think?
3. What is self-talk, and how do I use it?
4. Will God assist in my healing?

When I was through with my treatments, I became energized with the knowledge that I was going to recover. I would go in for a checkup, and the doctors would scope by throat and express amazement at how I was healing. I had no adverse side effects whatsoever. I got my taste back within a few weeks and celebrated my complete healing with family and friends at one of my favorite restaurants, eating all my favorite foods.

One of the most important concepts I had to learn in this healing process was how to change my way of thinking. You may be asking yourself, What does this theory have to do with me and healing my body? I believe it has everything to do with my healing! I realized that God had given me the various tools I needed to heal myself. Once I saw the connection between mind and body, I believe my mind sent out a signal of positive hope to my body, stimulating my health and well-being. I developed a new way of thinking. I believe it brought me health and vitality. God has given me many solutions through this thought process. I used them to bring God's wonderful blessings into my life. I hope they work for you too.

During the years that have followed my radiation treatments, I kept my faith in God, that He would heal me. I would never have cancer again. I meditated on God and His power. I knew beyond a shadow of a doubt that God had healed me. I had no doubts.

Each time that I went back for a checkup, I would tell my doctor to lighten up. He just knew the cancer would return. Finally after five years, I got him to smile and admit that through the healing powers of God, I had licked this cancer. My doctor and I knew the healing was from a higher power.

I believe it is imperative that I visualize and think only of a healthy body. If I concentrate on being sick, then I think the body will remain sick, since that is the predominant thought being fed to the body. I believe the state of my body is a reflection of my mind. I have spoken with many people that have gone through cancer treatments who picture themselves in a casket. What a negative idea to plant in the mind! I believe that is the very worst thing a cancer patient can do. When those pictures drifted into my mind, I knew I had to change my thoughts to healthy images. That is why I kept picturing myself in a healthy state.

Self-talk is so important. I had a friend with cancer. She told me that the only time she did not have cancer was when she was asleep. I wish she had told herself every waking moment that she was healthy in every way. I made a point of not even mentioning my disease. I believe that if you talk about your illness, then those are the predominant thoughts which the brain focuses on, and those negative thoughts will only bring more illness and disease into the body. Think healthy thoughts!

This thinking process is really based in faith. I believed, without any doubts, that God healed me. That left me with only healthy thoughts to fill my mind. I believe doubt is the enemy of faith. Walk by faith and vanquish doubt along with your illness.

The mind is the gateway to the body. Whatever the mind thinks or focuses on will become reality. I purposed to fill my mind with healing thoughts and good thoughts of the future. I did not allow my mind to journey down a negative path.
I think it is important to start planning for your future. Find your purpose and make plans to carry it out. Pray for guidance, and I believe God will show you the way. He did that for me. I fully believe, without any doubts, that God has shown me my purpose and I intend on doing everything possible to make that happen according to His will.

Words from the Wise

"The thing always happens that you really believe in; and the belief in a thing makes it happen."

—Frank Lloyd Wright

"To succeed, we must first believe that we can."

—Michael Korda

"That which dominates our imaginations and our thoughts will determine our lives. Therefore, it behooves us to be careful what we worship, for what we are worshipping we are becoming."

—Ralph Waldo Emerson

Healing Scriptures

"If you remain in me and my words remain in you, **ask whatever you wish, and it will be given you.**"

John 15:7 (NIV)

"'You will not have to fight this battle. Take up your positions; **stand firm and see the deliverance the LORD will give you**, O Judah and Jerusalem. Do not be afraid; do not be discouraged. Go out to face them tomorrow, and the LORD will be with you.'"

2 Chronicles 20:17 (NIV)

For as he **thinketh** in his heart, so is he.

Proverbs 23:7 (KJV)

I pray also that the eyes of your heart may be enlightened in order that you may know the hope to which he has called you, the riches of his glorious inheritance in the saints, and **his incomparably great power for us who believe.** That power is like the working of his mighty strength.

Ephesians 1:18–19 (NIV)

Steps I Used to Know That I Was Healed

- I held the knowledge that I was going to recover.
- I realized that I needed to change the way I thought.
- I realized that God gave me various tools to heal my body.
- I saw the connection between mind and body.
- I developed a new way of thinking.
- I meditated on God and His power daily.
- I only held thoughts of a healthy body.

Nine

The Miracle of Our Bodies

I searched for answers in the holistic realm of health:

1. Could I improve my diet to enhance my healing?
2. How could vitamins build up my immune system?
3. Are there any alternative methods to speed up my healing process?
4. How could I alleviate the pain in my shoulder?
5. What is energy healing?

I chose to make several physical changes in the way I regarded and honored the temple of my physical body during my time of healing.

Eating Right

I became very careful in what I ate. No more junk food. I tried to eat lots of vegetables and organic foods. I began to drink only organic milk. My wife would go to the farmers' market or get vegetables from her parents' garden. That is really the kind of food I love.

My maternal grandfather and grandmother always had a farm and a garden. When we would visit, my grandmother would always cook fabulous meals filled with fresh produce from her garden, and she always had fresh milk on the table. She also raised her own chickens, hogs, and cattle. Now that is living! I truly believe part of the reason for so much cancer today is the carcinogenic chemicals in the environment that get into our food. I do not think our bodies were meant to process these harsh chemicals. That is not how we were designed.

Vitamins:

I added vitamins to my daily regimen, after my radiation treatments, to help ensure my cells had the building blocks for healing. My doctors would not let me take any vitamins during my treatments because they would protect my cells—good and bad—from the radiation. This made me realize the importance of vitamins in my diet. If the vitamins protected my cells from radiation then, in my opinion, it made sense that they would protect my cells from other damaging influences such as free radicals.

I drank protein drinks by the carload, especially during the months when I could not stomach solid foods. I have always believed in protein drinks since they are an easy source of good protein, especially for breakfast.

Proteins:

Proteins aid the body by providing the building blocks that repair cells, tissues, bones, muscles, and blood. The amino acids from protein help the brain to function.

Proteins also affect hormones and enzymes that control all body processes. Proteins will prompt the brain to manufacture norepinephrine and dopamine, which promote alertness and give energy to the body.

Antioxidants and Free Radicals:

I started drinking juices rich in antioxidants. Certain vitamins are known to be rich in antioxidants, such as vitamins E and C. Free radicals form when the cells are not functioning properly or when our cells are bombarded with environmental factors such as radiation, poisons, cigarette smoke, etc. When I had my band, I probably sucked in more cigarette smoke than most people, singing in smoke-filled places. Once a free radical attacks one cell, they then go on to multiply and cause more damage. Healthy cells are constantly being attacked by free radicals, with age, the damage begins to accumulate. Antioxidants dissolve free radicals. According to scientific studies, free radicals cause long-term damage to cells, causing disease, stress on the immune system, and aging to the body overall.

I decided eating foods and drinking juices that combat free radicals was a great idea. When an antioxidant meets a free radical in the bloodstream, it naturally combines with it and coverts the free radical to water and oxygen. That's a good thing. If cellular damage lessens—health improves. I recommend that everyone seek out information on eating healthily during illness or recovery, and I continue the practice of eating healthily at all times. I believe in helping each of the cells in my body by eating foods that fight free radicals.

I worked with a man who had been diagnosed with melanoma (skin cancer). The doctors said that there was no known treatment to fight his cancer in this advanced state, and that he had about six months to live. When he went home and told his family the sad news, they stayed up all night praying to God for help. **Where do we go but to the Lord?** My colleague and his brother found an alternative health treatment in Mexico, so he took a leave of absence from work and travelled down there. Once there, he ate and drank only good foods, rich in antioxidants. When he came back home he was orange from drinking so much carrot juice, but when he went to his doctors his cancer cells had diminished. He kept up this regimen for a year and finally eliminated the cancer. In 2008 he celebrated six years of being cancer free.

I also met a preacher's wife who discovered she had breast cancer. Again the doctors told her there was no treatment for the kind of cancer she had, and gave her only a few months to live. She went to the elders of their church and in faith they prayed for her. She purchased a juicing machine and began a diet of juicing, drinking vegetables and fruits that had been processed through the juicer. She stayed on this diet for approximately six months. When she went back in to visit her doctor, the cancer was gone.

These two stories are true. I didn't mention names since they wanted to keep their privacy. I just wanted to tell my readers that there are alternative methods to cancer treatment. I personally chose to go the route that my medical doctor advised, but if I had been told that there was no treatment, then I am sure I would have tried these alternative treatments.

I truly believe that God healed the above people. It was their faith that took them on an alternative path directed by God. I believe God talks to us all the time, we just do not always listen or give Him the credit. Of course all good things come from God. All treatments that combat illnesses surely come from God and His great intelligence that He has loaned to man. I believe we are on the dawn of discovering a whole new way of approaching sickness and disease. Medical science is just now recognizing the ancient wisdom of how important the human mind and our belief systems are in the healing of the human body. I truly believe we will begin incorporating energy healing with the more traditional forms of medicine to a much larger extent.

Energy Healing via Reiki

During my radical surgery, the muscle that actually holds up my shoulder had been cut away from my neck because it was fused to a grouping of lymph nodes. My doctor told me that after surgery I would feel pain in my left shoulder, due to the fact that the muscle would fall down into my back. I heard of a Reiki master through a friend that was undergoing chemo therapy. She had been under Reiki therapy for her illness. I began Reiki therapy and found that it gave me much more mobility and relieved the pain in my shoulder.

Reiki (pronounced ray-key) is an ancient Japanese healing technique. It is a powerful therapy used for healing various health conditions, using energy from the therapist and God's energy. Reiki is based upon the theory that the human body is an energy form that can use its own energy plus God's energy for healing.

A Reiki practitioner connects to the universal energy of God and channels it to the recipient to remove any blockages and rebalance the energy within the body, eliminating disease in the process. Reiki reduces stress while promoting the feeling of well-being through mental and physical relaxation. It has been successful in relieving pain, cleansing the body of unhealthy toxins, balancing emotions, and cleansing the mind. It harmonizes well with other healing methods including orthodox medical treatments, massages, and natural health remedies. Reiki is not connected to any religion or cult. It simply uses the energy God has placed on this earth to heal our bodies. A key factor in Reiki healing is the belief and openness to receive the energy.

Healing Scriptures

"The LORD be exalted, who delights in the well-being of his servant."

Psalm 35:27 (NIV)

You who sit down in the High God's presence, spend the night in Shaddai's shadow, Say this: "GOD, you're my refuge. I trust in you and I'm safe!"

Psalm 91:1 (MSG)

Commit to the LORD whatever you do,
and your plans will succeed.

Proverbs 16:3 (NIV)

Words from the Wise

" . . . look to your health; and if you have it, praise God, value it next to a good conscience; for health is the second blessing that we mortals are capable of . . . "

—Izaak Walton

"The real doctor is the doctor within."

—Dr. Albert Schweitzer

Steps I Used to Promote Healing in My Body

- I chose to eat healthy foods.
- I started adding organic foods whenever possible.
- I added protein drinks to my diet.
- I added vitamins—especially vitamins E and C.
- I drank juices reach in antioxidants.
- I researched energy healing.
- I began Reiki treatments.

The Perfect Union of Science and God

I began searching for answers in science:

1. How does science affect my healing?
2. How does God manage His universe?
3. How does God's universe affect me?
4. Is there scientific evidence that can build my faith in God?
5. Do science and the Bible harmonize?
6. Could my negative thinking affect my health and world?

As my healing process unfolded, I found myself digging for answers in every aspect of my life. I sifted through my spiritual outlook and decided on a more positive approach. I gathered together the words of wise men and sages and was inspired to transform my thinking. I reduced stress factors; I changed what I ate. All of this led me to dig deeper into the science that might be at work in my body in tandem with my faith and the positive thinking in my mind and spirit. I wanted to know more about how the science of mind, body, spirit, and the Scriptures worked together or overlapped.

I began to read everything I could find on healing the body, mind, and spirit. I returned to my research of nutrition. I had a lot of past experience to lean on; for years I had sold vitamins and other nutritional supplements. I completely believed they had a part in my healing and recovery. I opened my mind to consider the healing powers of visualization, affirmations, and energy healing arts that I had never looked into before, like Reiki and Quantum Touch. I could see a connection between the mind and the healing of the body. I saw what the traditional medical world had to offer and decided that for me, there was more. I know that traditional medicine played a part in saving my life on more than one occasion, but I also discovered a new world of medicine that uses the power of the mind in the body's healing process.

In my quest for scientific theories that backed up this kind of healing, I found several interesting concepts presented by Dr. Wayne Dyer, Tony Robbins, and Deepak Chopra. All three of these best-selling authors have touched upon the same idea that our minds play a part in who we are and how we live. We draw into our worlds those things we think about most. This idea was new to me, and it led me to start asking scary questions: "Did I bring adversity into my life and to my family? Did my negative thoughts draw in negative results?" I also asked the question: "Is this thinking in line with the Bible, and do science and God harmonize with each other?"

I started looking at my moments of greatest adversity more closely. When I had my stroke, I was in a high-stress job. I literally worked night and day. I felt that I never could do enough to catch up on my work. I worried and worried, which drove my blood pressure higher and higher. I hate to admit it, but I am a perfectionist. To my way of thinking back then, nothing I could do was good enough. I was always dissatisfied with my world. So did I attract this adversity into my life and my family's life? I have come to believe that I did. I refused to go to the doctor for my blood pressure. I thought I could control it with diet and exercise, and yet I made no other changes to speak of. My pressure-cooker job and my negative thoughts were part of the picture I just did not realize were killing me.

The night I had my stroke, I was in the bathroom. My wife Mary woke up hearing me crashing into the walls. I was staggering around like a drunken man. Mary gave me a worried look and asked me if I was okay. I said, "Yes, just give me a second." Mary could see that the left side of my face was drawn—a sign of a stroke. She said that she was going to call an ambulance. I could not find my way safely out of my own bathroom, but neither would I admit there was something deadly wrong with me. "Just give me a second and I will be okay," I protested, in complete denial. Mary, wise woman, did not argue with me, she simply said, "Then lay down, before you fall." I did as she asked. Then Mary said, "Try to get up." I tried and tried to get up, but I couldn't find the strength or the ability. She called the ambulance.

The emergency room at the local hospital immediately ordered a CAT scan. The test showed that my right brain was bleeding. A small blood vessel had burst. Doctors thought that I would have to have surgery to stop the bleeding.

They immediately called CareFlight from Baylor Hospital in Dallas. My blood pressure shot up to 210/160 mmHG. Mary heard the doctors frantically calling CareFlight to ask them what medicine to give me. I lost consciousness.

Mary immediately started praying. She must have a direct line to God, or the Lord really wanted me to live. Within minutes I was in a helicopter on my way to Baylor Emergency Center in Dallas. Mary was told to call my parents and tell them that I was in a dire condition. They lived in Mississippi. It was one in the morning. The doctors knew I stood at Death's door. Mary called my parents and her brother to begin a night of prayers on my behalf.

When Mary got to Baylor Hospital, the amazing EMTs and emergency room doctors had stabilized my blood pressure. They decided to wait to see if the bleeding would stop on its own. Thank God and the savvy doctor who did not race to cut open my hard head, the bleeding had stopped. I did not have to have surgery. My belief is that my wife's quick thinking, my family's prayers, and a whole host of on-the-ball, middle-of-the-night medical personnel saved my life.

I spent nine months in rehab. At first I thought I could bounce back in just a few weeks, but it took me two weeks just to walk with help from the therapists. To walk on my own took four weeks. Then to actually do everything that I had been doing before my stroke meant a full nine months in therapy. That got me back to work, back to the same conditions that had put me in the hospital in the first place.

You see, even given the wake-up call of a near-death experience, I did not change my ways. I thought I was doing well. I had survived. I had overcome losses of motor function. I had worked hard. I had control over my blood pressure with prescription drugs. Then something else happened that shook my world. I lost my job at a company where I had worked for twenty-one years. Wow! What next? Well, five months later—cancer. My life was shaken to its very foundations. God uses such moments to reach us with His greatest truths. We turn to Him in our hours of need.

I questioned: What am I to do? How do I stop this chaos?

If we continue to question, a crisis can be our greatest opportunity to learn and grow as a soul. I was seeking answers. I was willing to grow, to embrace new ideas, to expand the understanding of my soul. I was drawn to further explore some of the scientific laws I had read about. A concept called the Law of Attraction kept coming to my attention in the new books I had been reading.

As I went through my process of healing, I studied more books on the laws of nature and the universal laws in science. I thought to myself: *Since the mind controls the body, I want to know as much as possible about any ideas that could strengthen my body in relation to the thought process*. This philosophy, called the Law of Attraction, gave me ideas I hoped might improve my health as well as other aspects of my life. The more I applied this theoretical law to my thinking, the healthier and happier I felt. I encourage you to try it. It is very powerful and fun.

I read the book *The Light Shall Set You Free* by Drs. Milanovich and McCune. They stated that there are basically twelve universal laws and twenty-one sub-laws that govern our universe. Some of the laws they mention are the Law of Gravity, Law of Vibration, Law of Polarity, and the Law of Attraction.

I used these philosophies as guidelines for my behavior. I feel that they enhanced my mental, physical, emotional, and spiritual health. In the humble opinion of this author, these ideas were, for me, gifts from God.

The philosophy of Milanovich and McCune is founded on their belief that everything in the universe is energy, including ourselves. So when I am speaking in terms of universal laws, I am talking about this philosophy of where my thoughts, feelings, words, and actions affect the energy around me which affects my healing process. I create my world.

> "Everything in the universe is energy, including us, and that energy moves in a circular fashion. At the microscopic level, we are a whirling mass of electrons and energy atoms . . ."
>
> **—Dr. Norma Milanovich and Dr. Shirley McCune**

One of the main reasons I was so excited about these theories is that they gave me hope that the power to change my destiny, my health, and my way of thinking was in my control. Of course, God has the ultimate control of His universe—my life and yours—but God allows us to make choices about how we think and live our lives. We choose. **I had a second chance for life.**

It is my belief that God structured His universe with specific laws that govern the operation of everything. These laws are sometimes referred to as Laws of Nature or Universal Laws. They are simply observations that people have made about how the universe operates. An example of one of these laws is gravity. The Law of Gravity states that all things with mass attract each other. Naturally, the object with the greatest mass has much more attractive power and pulls the other object to it. On earth, we know that things fall downward. This law has been in effect since the beginning of time and is universally true.

I believe that the Law of Attraction—"like attracts like"—joins in operation with the Law of Vibration. The Law of Vibration postulates that everything moves and vibrates. One of the reasons this made sense to me, with regard to my healing process, was that this idea applies to my mind and thoughts. If my thoughts create a vibration in the form of a frequency, I believe that this frequency of thought could attract good things into my life. Thus, my thoughts could be an important tool in helping my body to heal. I believe it is healing to think thoughts of health and give thanks. I believe this made a major difference in my recovery.

Scientific Quotes

"It is well known that the brain is an electrochemical organ; researchers have speculated that a fully functioning brain can generate as much as 10 watts of electrical power."

—Intelegen, Inc

"When you are attracted to another person it is likely that you and the other are in some sense vibrating in phase with each other . . . each of you is energized."

—Fred Alan Wolf, physicist

"Each molecule has its own frequency and receptors that tune into this frequency, much like a radio tunes into a particular station. This can occur even over vast distances."

—Lynn McTaggart, *The Field*

"The universe consists solely of waves of motion . . . there exists nothing other than vibration . . . principles that make sound into harmonious music are the same principles that govern all associating vibrations . . . "

—Walter Russell, *A New Concept of the Universe*

Law of Attraction: This philosophy, simply put, suggests that our thoughts, feelings, and words attract people and events into our lives because like energies attract. This idea and my faith helped me because I knew I was going to be okay, and I believed I could attract like forces in my life to support that belief. Doctors were telling me constantly that they were amazed at how fast I was healing with no side effects.

The Concept of Attraction and Vibration and the Word of God: Here are verses from the Bible that I believe demonstrate this concept of attraction.

> Summing it all up, friends, I'd say you'll do best by filling your minds and meditating on things true, noble, reputable, authentic, compelling, gracious—the best, not the worst; the beautiful, not the ugly; things to praise, not things to curse. Put into practice what you learned from me, what you heard and saw and realized. Do that, **and God, who makes everything work together,** will work you into his most excellent **harmonies.**
>
> **Philippians 4:8–9 (MSG)**

Think good thoughts and you will be in harmony with God's universe.

> "I tell you, love your enemies. Help and give without expecting a return. You'll never—I promise—regret it. Live out this God-created identity the way our Father

lives toward us, generously and graciously, even when we're at our worst. Our Father is kind; you be kind. Don't pick on people, jump on their failures, or criticize their faults— unless, of course, you want the same treatment. Don't condemn those who are down; that hardness can boomerang. **Be easy on people; you'll find life a lot easier. Give away your life; you'll find life given back, but not merely given back—given back with bonus and blessing. Giving, not getting,** is the way. **Generosity begets generosity.**"

Luke 6:35–38 (MSG)

"If your enemy is hungry, feed him; if he is thirsty, give him something to drink. In doing this, you will heap burning coals on his head." **Do not be overcome by evil, but overcome evil with good**.

Romans 12:20–21 (NIV)

Do good, and good will be attracted back to you.

I believe the feelings of love, contentment, and joy have the highest frequency or vibration. I believe that learning to feel love and contentment or joy helped to manifest my prayers and attracted the healing I wanted in my life. I believe it sped up my whole process of a healing reality.

I have spoken with many people that have questioned the existence of these laws and if they are from God. I began to study the life of Einstein, and what I found enhanced my faith in regard to the Word of God being in harmony with science and vice versa. This in turn anchored my belief system all the more by simple observation of the world around me, observation that God had provided all of us, his creation, a way of **hope** in this life. God gave us tools to use in our daily lives. Powerful tools. God wanted us to enjoy health and all good things.

"Determinism: The world obeys the precise laws discovered by science and, after the universe is set into motion, everything that happens is predetermined because the universe must obey these laws."

—Albert Einstein

For since the creation of the world His invisible attributes, His eternal power and divine nature, have been clearly seen, being understood through what has been made, so that they are without excuse.

Romans 1:20 (NASB)

Albert Einstein theorized that space and time are connected, and all matter is part of an energy field. I believe this **energy field** is God. The Bible speaks of God as the source of our very being. All matter, time, and space interact with each other, and once connected, each will affect the other forever by an invisible stream of energy—**God.**

"For in him we live and move and have our being."

Acts 17:28 (NIV)

Paul Davies wrote about these universal laws in his book *The Mind of God: The Scientific Basis for a Rational World.* Paul Davies is a professor of mathematical physics, author, and the winner of the 1996 Templeton Prize. Davies became interested in the concept of a unified science and religion after reading *Honest to God* by Anglican Bishop John T. Robinson. Davies tuned into the idea that God was sort of a "timeless ground of being."

What scientists keep trying to find is our source. Scientists, even Einstein, believed that there was order to our universe. They saw the evidence in the laws of nature, and some even saw them rooted in God.

"But if the divine underpinning of the laws is
removed, their existence becomes
a profound mystery."

—Paul Davies

The mystery of life astounds scientists, but they do see this order to our universe in the observations of these universal laws of nature. Scientists strive to explain in a rational way how our universe operates. They do not like to lean toward divine intervention or a creator of the universe. They have real problems seeing the source of everything when neither science nor mathematics can explain or see the source. Most scientists are visual people. They must see or at least be able to explain the source. That is where religious people come into view because they can see the source by faith.

Scientists have discovered through new technology that the base of all things is energy. When they look at the source of the smallest particle of the atom, a quark, they see nothing. At present there is little or no evidence of any structure to the quark. Therefore, the source of all matter is an unseen force—energy.

What Is Energy?

Merriam-Webster Dictionary Online defines it as "a usually positive spiritual force."

I looked up the word "energy" in several dictionaries to see how, as a people we define the concept of energy, and there in the current Merriam-Webster, as the third definition was: "a usually positive force." I had to smile. This seemed to me a perfect validation of my personal philosophy of life and healing.

Energy—an ever present form which is constantly moving in and out of form, and cannot be created or destroyed. This makes so much sense. God (energy) is constantly moving in and out of form in an ever present energy field that has been around forever and cannot be destroyed.

- So if God is energy and everything He created is energy, then how does it all work together?
- How do these laws affect my life?
- How does the Bible speak of these laws, and how am I to apply these laws to my way of thinking?

I began to feel my body strengthen and heal. I realized that I was made in the image of God and a part of Him was in me. I knew all I had to do was call upon Him and observe what He had given me to heal myself. I had the power of the universe at my fingertips. I believed this concept without question—no doubt. I encourage you to do the same.

Healing with God's Energy

Quantum physics was first discovered and talked about in the early 1900s by a man named Max Planck. He discovered a mathematical solution that showed energy is emitted and absorbed in small packets called quanta. Planck won the Nobel Prize in 1918. His quantum theory changed the world's perception of energy and the field of physics.

During the testing of the theory, scientists found that their thoughts could change the experiment they were involved with. Scientists witnessed that a **person's thoughts were actually causing a reaction in matter.** One of the most exciting discoveries of quantum physics is the realization that **our thoughts affect the world around us.** The power of thought literally enables us to affect reality by the way we think—good or bad. Our thoughts create a very powerful force.

Think of a simple atom which emits an electromagnetic field, or EMF. Then look at a molecule that emits a stronger EMF. Then take a large number of molecules that form a cell in the human brain, which contains at least 200 million such cells. All these cells emit thoughts that radiate energy into the universe through electromagnetic fields or EMFs.

The *American Heritage Dictionary* defines electromagnetic field, or EMF, as: "The field of force associated with electric charge in motion, having both electric and magnetic components and containing a definite amount of electromagnetic energy."

If all matter vibrates and produces frequencies, how about our brains?

If someone is in an accident and has a brain injury, the doctors usually perform a brain scan to determine if there are active brain signals or electrical activity. If there are no electrical activities in the brain, a person is said to be brain-dead. An electroencephalogram, or EEG, is the measurement of electrical signals in the brain, which sometimes are called brain waves. Our brain waves as a whole make up our consciousness, which determines our vibration and reflects with changes in frequency and amplitude of our brain waves.

Our brain waves are separated into different functions with different wave frequencies.

We can view and analyze the traces of electrical activity in the brain that represent each particular brain wave. All these brain waves have a different frequency measured in cycles per second or Hertz (Hz).

- **Beta** brain waves are measured at 13–40 Hz
- **Alpha** brain waves are measured at 7–13 Hz
- **Theta** brain waves are measured at 4–7 Hz
- **Delta** brain waves are measured at less than 4 Hz
- **Gamma** brain waves are measured at 40+ Hz.

I wanted to discuss brain waves in order to validate the point that the brain produces energy and vibrations which correlate to the universal law of vibration and attraction. Our thoughts actually affect the universe around us, our own bodies, and other people and things. Therefore, you can say that our thoughts determine our world as we view it.

What does all this brain information have to do with healing?

Scientists are researching the link between brain activity, physiology, and energy healing. The science of brain waves, combined with spirituality, is already yielding amazing results in the area of healing the body. It has been discovered that the Theta function of the brain is the barely conscious state present just before sleeping and just after waking. Theta is the border between the conscious and the subconscious mind. This state is the miracle state of problem solving, creativity, and accelerated healing.

Researchers have discovered that if we could meditate only ten minutes a day, we could relieve stress and heal our bodies from constant biological attacks of free radicals. Meditation usually involves the Theta part of our brain. In other words, we would be able to stop illnesses before they happen.

What heals our bodies? Our minds!

The entire purpose of this book is to give the reader **hope** based upon how I survived adversities, by using God's power and what God has given us through the laws of nature and the power of our minds. This approach to adversity is probably different from the old standard way of thinking, at least it is for me. I truly believe that God has given us all the tools to manage the world we live in, and of course we all have to realize we are in an ever-changing universe. I also believe that if we are to grow spiritually and physically we must change the way we look at things, which may involve changing our attitudes and beliefs. In a participatory universe of our own making, why would we expect that peace, healing, and a long and healthy life should be any more difficult to attain than to change our thinking.

This is how I believe part of my healing process worked:

- How I felt and thought actually created vibrations.
- God's universe corresponded in kind to the vibration created by these feelings.
- I changed my thoughts and feelings, linking them to a positive vibration.
- I am the creator of my own destiny—I choose to think correctly and follow God's Word. I decide.

How do I think these universal laws, the Law of Attraction and the Law of Vibration, work in my life?

- I believe I attract the energies that I think and feel.
- I believe spoken words carry that same energy, so what I say and what others say to me is very important.
- I believe I get what I ask for, according to God's will.
- Passionate commitment to my beliefs creates energy to fuel thought into action.
- My positive thoughts can be more powerful than my negative thoughts and feelings, so I am mindful of my thoughts and feelings.

I learned the following:

- God has set up universal laws that manage His universe.
- God's word harmonizes with science.
- Quantum physics has revealed that the thoughts of our subconscious and conscious mind are creating our experience of life.
- Energy is everywhere, and we can access this energy through our thinking.
- Energy is something that has always been and always will be coming in and out of form.

For everything comes from him and exists by his power
and is intended for his glory. All glory to him forever! Amen.

Romans 11:36 (NLT)

Steps I Used to Heal through Science:

- I studied how the laws of nature affect my life.
- I became aware of how my thoughts were affecting my health.
- I began to seek out answers.
- I was willing to grow spiritually.
- I applied the Law of Attraction to my healing by thinking positively.
- I attracted positive healing results.
- I concentrated my thoughts on love and joy, to attract good things like healing.
- I realized that God had given me tools to heal myself.
- I realized my mind was running the show in how my body healed.

Eleven

The Power of the Mind to Heal

I searched for information on how my mind works:

1. How can I use my mind to heal my body?
2. Does what I think affect my body?
3. How does my subconscious mind effect my healing?
4. How do I change how I think?

I believe this chapter is one of the most important, because I finally realized, in despair of my life, that my mind could have been my cure or my curse. I had to learn that my thoughts produced things, and that what I fed my mind is what would heal me or not.

Again I want to confess, I thought negatively for most of my life. I lived with thoughts of doom, despair, and curses. My heart was not always filled with love for my fellow man, despite God's instructions otherwise. Once I became aware of how my thoughts affected my life, then I chose to change them. I believe I did not begin to think positively or hopefully until I acknowledged that I needed to change the way I thought.

I knew my destiny, now how to keep my mind on that narrow and straight road?

I realized that I needed to be careful of what was in my subconscious and conscious mind. I realized that I was creating my realities. What I think drives me to perform activities in my life. My thoughts actually attract like thoughts from people in many different places. I knew that I needed to monitor what I was thinking constantly. I sure did not want to bring anything else negative into my life. When the mind decides to live, the body will follow with health to support the mind.

The Path to New Life: Clearing out My Old Way of Thinking

Since almost 80 percent of our thoughts come from the subconscious mind, I had to clean house, so to speak, on what was in my mind. I discovered that my subconscious mind is really running the show in my life most of the time! What I had to do was reprogram my subconscious mind to trust in God and not worry about what might happen. I have spent half my life worrying about what might happen. I worried so much that I actually brought what I was worrying about into my life as reality. I knew I had high blood pressure, but instead of doing something about it, I just worried about it. This resulted in a right brain bleed, a stroke, which resulted in paralyzing my left side completely. Also this worrying brought about loss of my job, cancer, and financial hardship.

I found that I was constantly thinking negative thoughts about people who I thought had wronged me somehow. I would dwell on those negative thoughts, which were hurting me physically or worse, mentally. I was causing future illnesses. Our minds were not designed to solve these problems. Only God can solve these problems. I discovered that I did not need to spend negative energy worrying about things I couldn't change.

Why worry so much about the economy? Can I change what is happening to oil prices or to the stock market?

I needed to live for God, trusting that He will always take care of me. That way I do not put those negative thoughts into my mind, causing me stress and disease. Stress is the number one killer in America. Stress has been linked to cancer, heart disease, high blood pressure, and the list goes on and on. It only makes sense that our minds were not designed to handle all this worry and fear. That is why our creator told us over and over again to not worry about anything. We should trust Him to take care of us.

Remember God controls all things. I realized that I needed to turn to God and let Him handle all the situations or people over which I had no control. After I had my stroke and cancer, I realized that whatever came my way God could and would handle it. **I had to surrender to God what belonged to Him, and what belongs to Him is my entire life.** When adversity comes along, I give it to God and do my part, which is to simply **believe** He can handle anything.

I also live my life with thankfulness every day. I wake up in the morning and thank God for feeling good. I am thrilled to be able to work. I think that thankfulness is one of the most important things to start out your day, filling your subconscious with positive statements. Say things out loud so that your subconscious hears them and takes them in.

Let go of limiting factors.

I have learned to believe and let go of limiting factors. When things or people overwhelm my thinking and keep me from depending on God, I manage to segregate those thoughts. When a person or event, that I have absolutely no control of, troubles me in my life, I visually place that person or event into a room, closing and locking the door and giving the key to God.

Of course, this is just visualization, but it is as real as if I were standing right in front of the person. Your thoughts make your reality. Once you have turned these problematic thoughts over to God, you are free of them and can relieve that stress from your mind. Believe me, this works. I do it all the time. I then am free to think only good thoughts that bring only good things into my life, not the bad things of the past that I brought into my mind by worrying or stressing over things, people, or events that I had no control over.

In the past, I would spend hours or days reliving all the bad experiences that I had in my life. Statements that people had said to me that had hurt my feelings or events that had occurred that caused me to feel downtrodden filled with negative thoughts. These thoughts actually made me sick through depression.

Our minds control our bodies.

Healing Scriptures

Don't fret or worry. Instead of worrying, pray. Let petitions and praises shape your worries into prayers, letting God know your concerns. Before you know it, a sense of God's wholeness, **everything coming together for good**, will come and settle you down. It's wonderful what happens when **Christ displaces worry** at the center of your life.

Philippians 4:6–7 (MSG)

God is love. When we take up permanent residence in a life of love, **we live in God and God lives in us.** This way, love has the run of the house, becomes at home and mature in us, so that we're free of **worry** on Judgment Day—our standing in the world is identical with Christ's. **There is no room in love for fear.** Well-formed love banishes fear. Since fear is crippling, a fearful life—fear of death, fear of judgment—is one not yet fully formed in love.

1 John 4:17–18 (MSG)

For God has not given us a **spirit of fear and timidity, but of power, love, and self-discipline.**

2 Timothy 1:7 (NLT)

"Indeed, the very hairs of your head are all numbered. Don't be afraid; you are worth more than many sparrows."

Luke 12:7 (NIV)

"Look at the birds of the air; they do not sow or reap or store away in barns, and yet your heavenly Father feeds them. Are you not much more valuable than they?"

Matthew 6:26 (NIV)

"Therefore I tell you, whatever you **ask for in prayer, believe that you have received it, and it will be yours.**"

Mark 11:24 (NIV)

Words from the Wise

"The mind is its own place, and in itself
can make heaven of Hell, a hell of Heaven."

—John Milton

"Beliefs in limits, creates limited people."

—Tony Robbins, *Unlimited Power*

"The human mind is our fundamental resource."

—John F. Kennedy

"It is psychological law that whatever we desire to accomplish we must impress upon the subjective or subconscious mind."

—Orison Swett Marden

"All the resources we need are in the mind."

—Theodore Roosevelt

"Our subconscious mind contains such power and complexity that it literally staggers the imagination."

—John Kehoe

"The reason why curing cancer by yourself is a miracle but mending a broken arm is not comes down to the mind-body connection."

—Deepak Chopra, M.D.

A broken bone is automatically healed by our immune system, which is controlled by our subconscious mind. This is part of the auto-healing process that is programmed into our bodies. To heal something like cancer, our minds have to be engaged. The same immune system can heal cancer, just as it heals a broken bone, but it has to be prompted by our minds. The subconscious mind controls bodily functions such as breathing, heart rate, and the immune system, and it performs 24/7. It is dominant during sleep and always open to the power of suggestion. If your conscious mind makes the affirmation that you are healing, your subconscious mind will eventually accept this as fact and heal the body. The reverse is also true: if you think you are dying, then your subconscious mind prepares for death.

Our bodies are constantly producing new cells. I often wondered: If I am replacing cells constantly, then why does an illness seem to progress even though I am getting fresh new cells? I believe that if my mind is telling my body that it is sick with something like cancer or heart disease, then the new cells carry that information, which in turn creates new sick cells. All of this is controlled at the subconscious level. I also believe that if we are telling our body that it is healthy, then our bodies will create new healthy cells.

Use the visualization process to instruct your cells to be healthy. **Your mind controls your body.**

I believe God has given us an infinite intelligence which goes beyond our conscious intellect.

Can you comprehend the intelligence that goes into controlling all the functions of our body? Controlling the heartbeat alone is simply beyond my understanding. On average, the heart of an adult beats about seventy-two times a minute—103,680 times in a day—37,843,200 times in a year. For most healthy people those heartbeats are in perfect rhythm, never missing a beat.

I came to believe in this miracle-working power of my subconscious mind, which reaffirmed my belief that truly anything is possible.

God is my creator and did not give me a spirit of limitation but of immeasurable possibilities!

Managing What Is in Our Subconscious Mind

Researchers have stated that we have more than 50,000 thoughts a day. We are motivated to act a certain way based on our memory of our past experiences. For example, if a child touches an iron and burns himself, it is unlikely that he will ever purposefully touch an iron again. The memory of his experience creates a fear of getting burned, which will impact his future behavior. All such memories are managed by the subconscious mind.

There are two ways that the mind is fed information—consciously and subconsciously. The information that we purposefully put in our mind comes from many sources such as: books, seminars, educational audio/visual programs, formal education, etc. The information that has been fed to our minds at an unconscious level since birth also comes from a variety of sources. Some of these include our parents or guardians, our teachers, and society at large. We are constantly bombarded with messages from our environment which actually then create our belief systems.

What is a belief system anyway? Simply put, a belief system is a group of thoughts that you believe to be true. You can hold these beliefs at a conscious or subconscious level. The ones that you have at a conscious level are ones that you can articulate and recognize how they motivate your actions. For example, you may have a conscious belief that if you work hard and save money you will have a comfortable retirement. You know this is what you believe, so you work hard and try to save money to support that belief.

As children, our mothers and fathers read stories to us that started our belief systems. Growing up, I had a wonderful neighbor who had lost two babies to crib death. When I was born she sort of adopted me. Her name was Tess Houser, and she would read me Bible stories over and over again. This started my first belief system. Also, my dad is a gospel preacher, and I have sat at his feet many, many times while he was studying what he was to preach next. I asked a million questions, and Dad would always answer me by the Bible. My belief system!

So what we believe to be true in our conscious minds and what we fear in our sub-conscious minds determines how we perceive reality. These beliefs can empower us to perform extraordinary things or they can cripple us to failure.

One of my favorite true life stories is about Roger Bannister who was a famous athlete for being the first person to break the four-minute mile run. A feat thought by many to be impossible. On May 6, 1954, the Englishman Roger Bannister ran the first sub-four-minute mile in recorded history, with a time of 3 minutes 59.4 seconds at the Iffley Road Track in Oxford, England. In the last fifty years the four-minute barrier has been lowered by almost seventeen seconds. Still, it remains the standard by which all male amateur milers, including American college milers, are measured.

This true life story goes to show all of us that we can limit ourselves by past experiences or faulty reasoning, and miss out on great victories.

Another true life story: My wife, Mary Beth, had a very serious accident when she was eleven years old. She and her family went on their very first vacation that she could remember. The first night they camped at a site just inside the Missouri border, and she and her brother immediately decided to go mountain climbing. When she was about sixty feet up the mountain, she decided that she didn't want to go any further. When she started back down the mountain she somehow got to going too fast and ended up falling down the mountain until she landed on a jagged rock. Of course it wasn't the fall that was the problem but the sudden stop. She had a head injury which made her temporarily blind but no other visible signs of injury were known.

Her family took her to a local hospital, but the doctors could not determine why she was in so much pain. The accident had happened on a Thursday night. By Saturday she was much worse. Her mom and dad made the decision to fly her back to Paris, Texas, where local doctors recognized immediately that she had internal injuries. She was transported to St. Paul's Hospital in Dallas where doctors performed exploratory surgery on Saturday night to repair a burst liver and severed kidney. She had suffered under those conditions for two days and lost almost all her blood, but she survived. In and of itself, this was a miracle. God had intervened.

Even more amazing was that this happened in 1964, a time when there had not been a single successful liver surgery. If it had not been for a very brave young doctor by the name of Dr. Ernest Poulas, who did not limit his mind to past experiences, she would have died. Dr. Poulas had just experienced a failed liver surgery of a good friend's child who had ruptured his liver in a bicycle accident, falling on the handle bars. Because Dr. Poulas did not have a limited way of thinking, Mary Beth recovered from the surgery where they removed three-fourths of her liver. She not only recovered, but they learned that the liver can regenerate itself within approximately nine months. The two things that Mary Beth remembers were praying to God and her father saying that she was going to be okay—her belief system telling her body to heal.

If we do not learn to change the way we think, then we will live a limited life or worse, die from a limited mind.

So I began asking myself, How I can tap in to this universe of energy that uses all thoughts to create reality? How can I change my mind to expect unlimited favor from God and to live an unlimited life?

I found that when I used the tools discussed previously about affirmations, visualization, and prayer, I began to change my thoughts. I started repeating the things that I had prayed over and over until my mind accepted them as reality. **I was diligent to believe I had already received the prayers.**

> "**Have faith in God**," Jesus answered. "I tell you the truth, if anyone says to this mountain, 'Go, throw yourself into the sea,' and does not doubt in his heart but believes that what he says will happen, it will be done for him. Therefore I tell you, whatever you ask for in prayer, **believe that you have received it, and it will be yours.**"
>
> **Mark 11:22–24 (NIV)**

I monitored how I was feeling, thus becoming aware of my constant thoughts. When I felt energized and confident, then I realized that my subconscious mind was using the positive facts that I had been feeding it. Over time, these positive influences had a greater and greater effect over the negative ones since my subconscious mind only recalls what has been programmed into it. The subconscious mind knows no reasoning, just the facts.

I started to say affirmations to put those prayer requests into my subconscious.

I used the "I AM" process. God speaks of himself as "I AM."

I thought of God as the I AM:

I AM your provider of all things.

I AM your healer.

I AM your answer to all your needs.

Then I thought of myself as an I am:

I am a person with vibrant health.

I am a loving person that is loved.

I am happy and content.

I am thankful to God Almighty.

Or the "I can" declaration of faith:

I can do all things through Christ.

I can heal my body through God's energy.

Visualize—I Create My Reality:

I have pictures on my desk and on the walls around my desk which keep my subconscious mind focused on the things I want to bring into my life. I suggest you do the same thing—it can be a house, a car, a person, a job, or anything that you can possibly dream of attaining. I created a healing book that has all my dreams laid out so that I can visualize them day after day until they become my reality.

When I was in rehab after my stroke, my therapists would tell me to surround myself with pictures of where I wanted to end up. This would keep my mind and energy focused on the outcome. I wanted to have vibrant health and be surrounded by the people I loved. So I set out pictures of past vacations where I was healthy and happy. These pictures kept me going. Today if you could see me playing tennis with my son, you would swear I had never had a stroke that completely paralyzed my left side to where I forgot I had a left arm or leg. I would have to look at my hand to move it just inches. Nor could you picture when I lost fifty pounds during my cancer treatment and looked like death warmed over. With God all things are possible, because today I have vibrant health.

God can do anything, you know—far more than you could ever **imagine or guess or request in your wildest dreams!** He does it not by pushing us around but **by working within us, his Spirit deeply and gently within us.**

Ephesians 3:20 (MSG)

Expect the prayers to be fulfilled. I would think of the process of when Mary Beth and I were expecting our baby boy, Brandon. The doctor told us that we were going to have a baby, but we hadn't seen the baby yet. In our subconscious minds, we knew that our doctor tested Mary for pregnancy with a 100 percent certainty. All of us have been programmed to believe whatever our doctors tell us. Therefore, we never questioned the fact that Mary was pregnant after her doctor's visit. We knew she was pregnant. We started buying baby clothes and baby furniture and so on. We had made the reality in our minds. We were expecting a baby!

The same way we know to expect a baby because the doctor has told us that we were going to have a baby, is the same way I know when I pray to God that He will fulfill my requests. I became expectant. I looked for the answered prayers. I prepared for the answered prayers. I also knew that sometimes it might take some time to pull things together, but eventually I knew they would become my reality.

Expect God's Favor!

I realized that my mental outlook was going to determine how I lived my life. I also realized that I was not perfect, but that God had taken care of my imperfections through Christ, sacrificing His life for me.

Love is the highest frequency—I began to concentrate on things that made me feel loved or good. When I pet my dog Sam, I feel love. When I think of Jesus dying on the cross for my sins, I think of great love. Thoughts like these are what will attract good things back to you.

Faith, hope and love. But the greatest of these is love.

1Corinthians13:13 (NIV)

My dear children, let's not just talk about love; **let's practice real love.** This is the only way we'll know we're living truly, living in God's reality. It's also the way to shut down debilitating self-criticism, even when there is something to it. For God is greater than our worried hearts and knows more about us than we do ourselves.

1 John 3:18–20 (MSG)

How I Tapped into the Power of the Mind:

- I changed my predominant thoughts to a positive nature.
- I eliminated negative self-talk.
- I reprogrammed my subconscious mind to think positively.
- I was thankful for all my blessings.
- I dreamed big—way beyond my abilities.
- I asked God for my every need.
- I believed in God and His power.

Twelve

Spiritual Growth—the Purpose of Adversity

I began asking questions about my purpose in life:

1. What does God want me to do?
2. What have I learned from my adversities?
3. Did God want me to be sick or impoverished?
4. Where was my hope?

The question which comes to mind is, why write a book on adversity? Was this my destiny, my purpose? For me, that question was answered in the spring of 2006. I was listening to a radio talk show when a man called in. I could tell his voice was quivering and gasping for air as he explained to the host of the show that he needed to talk to him about his wife who was dying of cancer. The host of course told the man to hang on the phone and he would discuss this issue with him off the air. When I heard the complete desperation and frustration in the man's voice I wept. As the old saying goes, I felt his pain because I too had been down that road. I too had felt despair and doom—**no hope.** I determined that day that I would write a book that would help people conquer the faith issue in their minds and give them **hope**. I pray that people with adversities of all kinds can be helped by what I have learned.

Yes, I, Wally Hogland had cancer and am now totally healed. I knew I could help a person like the one that had called in because I knew all the emotions a person goes through when they are dealing with cancer or any life-threatening situation—**adversity**, if you will. I want all of you reading this book to know that God has made you and knows everything about you. He loves us more than we could ever know, and He longs to help us.

> Oh yes, you shaped me first inside, then out; you formed me in my mother's womb. I thank you, High God—you're breathtaking! Body and soul, I am marvelously made! I

> worship in adoration—what a creation! You know me inside and out, you know every bone in my body; you know exactly how I was made, bit by bit, how I was sculpted from nothing into something. Like an open book, you watched me grow from conception to birth; all the stages of my life were spread out before you, the days of my life all prepared before I'd even lived one day.
>
> **Psalm 139:14 (MSG)**

I also realized that I had a purpose in life to fulfill. I read Rick Warren's book, *A Purpose Driven Life*, which drove me to begin writing mine. I believe we all have great purposes that God has given to us. He has made us perfect and has given us all the ability to carry out our purposes. I feel that I have lived fifty-five years to come to this point in my life to share what I have learned with you. I found that there is hope and not despair and not just life, but an abundant life. I had to actually experience all the things that I am writing about before I could have the insight on the solution.

I have lived my life blaming others for my shortcomings. I filled my heart with hate and resentment. If things went wrong in my life, I found someone that caused it. Of course, this was all a lie perpetrated by Satan himself. He is always just around the corner, waiting for us to invite him in, and we all do sometimes in our lives. I felt powerless and at times hopeless. I felt I was doomed! In fact, I know there are a lot of you out there that feel the same way. Some days I questioned why I was even born.

Since I spent all my energy thinking on bad or negative thoughts, I brought sickness and financial hardships into my life and my family's life. It took me many years after my stroke, losing my job, and cancer to realize where the power existed to change my destiny.

If we all pay attention, God directs our paths. We just have to listen, ask, and believe.

During my recovery years I put my faith in God, that He would heal me, and that I would never have cancer again. I told myself each day that I came from a very big God and was made perfect in His image. I meditated on God and His power. I knew beyond a shadow of a doubt that God had healed me. I had no doubts.

I finally realized that God did not want to punish me, but He wanted me to come to Him so that He could provide for me. He nudged me to try and wake me up. Again, if we do not ask for His help, He cannot help us. I also realized that someone else could not bring God into my life. I had to do it. Then to invoke His power, **I had to believe without any doubt** that He would do what I asked, according to His will. It is that simple.

Believe without any doubt.

But when he asks, he must **believe and not doubt**, because he who doubts is like a wave of the sea, blown and tossed by the wind. That man should not think he will receive anything from the Lord; he is a double-minded man, unstable in all he does.

James 1:6–8 (NIV)

So that you can see exactly what it is **he is calling you to do**, grasp the immensity of this glorious way of life he has for his followers, oh, **the utter extravagance of his work in us who trust him—endless energy, boundless strength**!

Ephesians 1:19 (MSG)

I also believe we all have a purpose in life, and I believe one of my many purposes is to share with the world what I have discovered. You may say that there have been many, many people that have discovered this very fact, and I absolutely agree with you. However, I have been near death, in the hospital twice, and I have to tell you all, there are thousands and thousands of people that do not know this source of hope. I saw and talked to many people who felt that they had none. My goal is to show them the hope!

Scriptures of Hope

But those who **hope** in the LORD will renew their strength. They will soar on wings like eagles; they will run and not grow weary, they will walk and not be faint.

Isaiah 40:31 (NIV)

For everything that was written in the past was written to teach us, so that through endurance and the encouragement of the Scriptures we might have **hope.**

Romans 15:4 (NIV)

The widow who is really in need and left all alone puts her **hope** in God and continues night and day to pray and to ask God for help.

1 Timothy 5:5 (NIV)

> I pray also that the eyes of your heart may be enlightened in order that you may know the **hope** to which he has called you, the riches of his glorious inheritance in the saints, and his incomparably great power for us who believe. That power is like the working of his mighty strength.
>
> **Ephesians 1:18–19 (NIV)**

Unfortunately, there are not many doctors who have the belief that God can and will help man on earth. They tell you that you have no hope. I have talked to many people who have been told by their doctors that they have only months to live. Says who? I can tell you they do not know this! They think they do, but I know they do not. They go by statistics, which, in God's world, means nothing. If I went by statistics, I would not be here on earth writing this book, nor would my wife be alive. My doctors have told me that I should not have made it through the stroke or the cancer, statistically speaking.

I have believed in God since I was a small boy, but I never had the ultimate faith to live in His power. Somehow I thought He was up in heaven and didn't want to be bothered by little ole' lowly me. I was wrong. He is waiting for everyone to come to the knowledge that He holds all life, in this world and the next.

I also want to tell you that I have changed 180 degrees from where I was ten years ago. I have to confess that I was a negative thinker. I would dwell on things people said which hurt me. I couldn't get them out of my mind. Thoughts would torment me and keep me from living in peace. Gradually, with the help of Tony Robbins, Dr. Dyer, Joel Osteen, and, of course, God, I have changed my thinking process. If I start to think on something negative, I recognize the thought process and change it to something good and positive. I have also learned that if you do something consistently for thirty days, you can change old habits of living and thinking. When you come to the point of recognizing when you start to think negative thoughts, then you finally have the ability to control your world.

We are what we think.

I do a little substitute teaching for a high school. One day I came into a classroom and looked for what the teacher had left me to teach that day. On the desk was the film *The Secret*. The note said to show this to the students and have them take notes. Well, the person taking the notes was me. After school,

Words from the Wise

"Nothing in your life is arbitrary. It's all for a purpose."

—Rick Warren

"God never does anything accidentally and he never makes mistakes. He has a reason for everything he creates."

—Rick Warren

"Change your thoughts and you change your world."

—Norman Vincent Peale

I went directly to the bookstore and purchased it. That night my wife and I watched the movie again. Mary Beth and I both looked at each other and said, "I finally get it." Again, God was leading us through this whole awakening process.

The Secret put things into explanations that we could understand. I really enjoyed and got so much from this movie. In a few weeks I was in a discussion about the power of the Law of Attraction. I asked the ladies there if they had seen *The Secret*. One lady said, "That is all humanistic and against God's Word." I did not argue with this lady, but I purposed in my heart that I would include the scientific facts into my book to show how

God designed His universe using laws of nature—laws that govern how we live on this earth and how the Bible is in total harmony with these scientific theories.

Steps I Used to Find My Purpose:

- I searched for God's purpose in my adversities.
- I realized that God wanted me to help others.
- I purposed in my heart to share my healing steps with others.
- I realized that God did not want to punish me but to help me.
- I changed my thinking and my life to reflect God's will.
- I realized that I had become what I thought about most.
- I searched out new philosophies.

Thirteen

Weary and Heavy-Laden

I questioned whether I had the faith to endure:

1. How can I have enough strength to go on?
2. How can I make it through the treatments?
3. How can I lean on the Lord and not myself?
4. How can I build my faith to heal myself?
5. How can I tell my body to keep on fighting?

At the end of my cancer treatments I didn't think I could go on. I had lost fifty pounds and was so weak and tired of doctors and hospitals. I am sure there are many of you that can relate to this condition. I think it was about my thirty-second radiation treatment when I went into my oncologist's office and said I couldn't go on. I was ready to call it quits and get into a healing state. He sat me down and told me that if I quit early I might be risking the cancer coming back. Statistically speaking, the forty treatments had been shown to have the best results. He talked me in to going on, so I went home each day after the treatments and prayed to God for strength. How could I endure much more of this pain and anguish? I had a friend going through chemo for another kind of cancer, and she would get so tired and weary that she just wanted to give up. I am writing this chapter to encourage you to keep up the fight and not let your guard down.

I kept telling myself that this was just a period of time and it too would pass. I just had to make it through a few more days, and then I could start my recovery. I sometimes felt that the treatment was harder on the body, mind, and spirit than the disease. When I felt too weak to go on I would think of Jesus praying in the garden of Gethsemane. Christ knew that He would carry upon His shoulders the sins of the world, separating Him temporarily from God, which put Him in deep anguish.

He pulled away from them about a stone's throw, knelt down, and prayed, "Father, remove this cup from me. But please, not what I want. What do you want?" At once an angel from heaven was at his side, strengthening him. He prayed on all the harder. Sweat, wrung from him like drops of blood, poured off his face.

Luke 22:42–46 (MSG)

Jesus knows what anguish men have to go through on earth since He was beaten and crucified for us. He can empathize with our pain. Lean on Jesus!

May God give you strength to endure and greater faith each day. You are much stronger than you know. The road is long, but the victory is sure! I pray that the victory will be soon.

Words from the Wise

"We must all face the test given us by God with positive attitudes and grasp the limitless possibility. When we do so, we . . . conquer and rule over our circumstances."

—Dr. David Yonggi Cho

"In the depth of winter, I finally learned that there was within me an invincible summer."

—Albert Camus

"Love the moment. Flowers grow out of dark moments . . . each moment is vital. It affects the whole. Life is a succession of such moments, and to live each, is to succeed."

—Corita Kent

Again for strength and peace, I turned to the Scriptures to let the Word soothe my soul.

Scriptures to Help Our Faith and Give Us Strength to Endure

"Come to me, all you who are weary and burdened, and I will give you rest."

Matthew 11:28 (NIV)

Do you not know? Have you not heard? The LORD is the everlasting God, the Creator of the ends of the earth. He will not grow tired or weary, and his understanding no one can fathom. He gives strength to the weary and increases the power of the weak."

Isaiah 40:28–29 (NIV)

Those who know your name will trust in you, for you, LORD, have never forsaken those who seek you.

Psalm 9:10 (NIV)

I look up to the mountains; does my strength come from mountains? No, my strength comes from God, who made heaven, and earth, and mountains.

Psalm 121:1–2 (MSG)

So let God work his will in you. Yell a loud no to the Devil and watch him scamper. Say a quiet yes to God and he'll be there in no time. Quit dabbling in sin. Purify your inner life. Quit playing the field. Hit bottom, and cry your eyes out. The fun and games are over. Get serious, really serious. Get down on your knees before the Master; it's the only way you'll get on your feet.

James 4:7–10 (MSG)

> You do not have, because you do not ask God. When you ask, you do not receive, because you ask with wrong motives, that you may spend what you get on your pleasures.
>
> **James 4:2–3 (NIV)**
>
> But the fruit of the Spirit is love, joy, peace, patience, kindness, goodness, faithfulness, gentleness and self-control. Against such things there is no law.
>
> **Galatians 5:22–23 (NIV)**

Steps I Used to Build My Faith and Increase My Stamina:

- I meditated on God's Word.
- I leaned on God's power.
- I focused on God's strength, not my weakness.
- I prayed for strength and patience.
- I watched Joel Osteen's sermons on adversity.
- I stated the affirmation "This too shall pass."

Fourteen

Victory and Abundance

I began questioning what God wanted for me:

1. Does God want me to be sick?
2. Does God want me to have financial hardships?
3. Is it God's will for Christians to be poor financially?
4. Does God want good things and blessings for His children?

As I was in my healing state after all my treatments, I began to think of myself as a victor and not a victim. I praised God's name for giving me the healing energy that I know can only come from Him. I realized that when I leaned on the Lord through my adversity, I could then look forward to God restoring my health and my world.

It gives me great joy and comfort to look at how God blesses His children and how He has purposes for all of us. I would read passages every day in my healing book, which would make me hopeful of a full recovery and an abundant life filled with God's blessings.

> You prepare a feast for me in the presence of my enemies. You honor me by anointing my head with oil. **My cup overflows with blessings.**
>
> **Psalm 23:5 (NLT)**

David, in Psalm twenty-three, is stating a fact that his world was overflowing from God's blessings. Did David have adversities in his life? Yes, just as we do, but with God on his side his life was blessed. David was not always perfect in the eyes of God, but God loved David because his heart was always penitent. David made mistakes, but he would always come back in alignment with God. David was a passionate man with great faith. He had a purpose and he lived it. He lived through the power of God. This is exactly what God wants from us. We need to be like David and expect God's blessings by living through His power.

I want to live with God as my God!

"I will live with them and walk among them, and **I will be their God, and they will be my people.**"

2 Corinthians 6:16 (NIV)

I also have spoken to many Christian leaders who say we shouldn't listen to people who preach health and wealth. I believe that God wants the very best for His children and not the worst. God lives in a world where there is abundance, beauty, joy, happiness, and no sickness. Well, my Christian friends say that we do not live in heaven yet, but that life will be there for us when we die. I have to disagree with them to a certain extent. I believe we create our world through our thoughts. If we think on good things, as God has directed, He will send us good things, blessings. Examples of those blessings are found in the Old Testament.

But remember the LORD your God, for **it is he who gives you the ability to produce wealth**, and so confirms his covenant, which he swore to your forefathers, as it is today.

Deuteronomy 8:18 (NIV)

The LORD will grant you abundant prosperity—in the fruit of your womb, the young of your livestock and the crops of your ground—in the land he swore to your forefathers to give you.

Deuteronomy 28:11 (NIV)

When God made his promise to Abraham, he backed it to the hilt, putting his own reputation on the line. He said, **"I promise that I'll bless you with everything I have—bless and bless and bless!"**

Hebrews 6:13 (MSG)

God blessed Abraham both on earth and in heaven, and I believe He blesses us on earth and in heaven.

Can you only imagine everything God has? God promised not only life but an abundant life, full of whatever we need. Remember, God lives on streets of gold!

Yes, God promised Abraham that through him would come a great nation with God as their God. We are that nation, we who believe in God's son, Jesus. We are God manifested. God dwells in each of His children, and lives each day with them.

You parents—if your children ask for a loaf of bread, do you give them a stone instead? Or if they ask for a fish, do you give them a snake? Of course not! So if you sinful people know how to give good gifts to your children, how much more will your heavenly **Father give good gifts** to those who **ask him**.

Matthew 7:9–11 (NLT)

Quit worrying about whether you are bothering God. You are not. He longs to walk with you every moment of every day. Yes, you, little ole' you! He loves each and every one of us. In fact, He loved us so much that He gave His only begotten son to die for our sins. Now that is love! So come boldly to God and ask Him for help. He is there just waiting. I learned to

Scriptures of God's Promise

"And so I tell you, keep on asking, **and you will receive what you ask for.** Keep on seeking, and you will find. Keep on knocking, and the door will be opened to you. For everyone who asks, receives. **Everyone who seeks, finds. And to everyone who knocks, the door will be opened."**

Luke 11:9–10 (NLT)

May those who delight in my vindication shout for joy and gladness; may they always say, "The LORD be exalted, **who delights in the well-being of his servant."**

Psalm 35:27 (NIV)

Abraham named the place Yahweh-Yireh (which means "the LORD will provide"). To this day, people still use that name as a proverb: "On the mountain of the **LORD it will be provided."**

Genesis 22:14 (NLT)

So here's what I want you to do, God helping you: **Take your everyday,** ordinary life—your sleeping, eating, going-to-work, and walking-around life—**and place it before God as an offering**. Embracing what God does for you is the best thing you can do for him. Don't become so well-adjusted to your culture that you fit into it without even thinking. Instead, fix your attention on God. You'll be changed from the inside out. Readily recognize what he wants from you, and quickly respond to it. Unlike the culture around you, always dragging you down to its level of immaturity, **God brings the best out of you**, develops well-formed maturity in you.

Romans 12:1–2 (MSG)

Whenever, though, they turn to face God as Moses did, God removes the veil and there they are—face-to-face! They suddenly recognize that God is a living, personal presence, not a piece of chiseled stone. And when **God is personally present, a living Spirit, that old, constricting legislation is recognized as obsolete. We're free of it! All of us**! Nothing between us and God, our faces shining with the brightness of his face. And so we are transfigured much like the Messiah, **our lives gradually becoming brighter and more beautiful as God enters our lives and we become like him.**

2 Corinthians 3:16–18 (MSG)

not limit God in my thinking. Ask God for His blessings and abundance that is just waiting for us.

God wants His children to lead a wonderfully free and happy life. He wants the very best for us, but He knows what is good for us and what might cause harm. That is why He tells us not to be obsessed with this world. We should keep everything in perspective, and above all, keep Him first in our lives. Keep God at the center of your life.

I want to become like Christ!

An abundant life is not all about money. Abundance, to me, is having God by my side, lots of love from my family, vibrant health, financial freedom to be able to help my family and others, abounding wisdom to share with fellow Christians, and an abundance of thanksgiving. This is the life God has promised for His children.

God does not want His children to have hardships or adversities. Since we live in a world filled with adversities of all kinds, it is imperative that we have connections to the source that can pull us through these adversities. God tells us over and over again to ask Him for help. **If we do not have, it is because we do not ask**. God has all power but will not do anything to intervene on earth unless someone asks Him to. He will never force His own will upon anyone. We have the key, so to speak, on the activation of God's power. **We simply have to ask**. I learned really quickly that asking was simple. The hard part was the faith to know that God will do what we ask. That went against all that I had believed for fifty years. I just didn't have the knowledge or the faith to expect God's favor. Wow, was I wrong!

"Therefore I tell you, whatever you **ask for in prayer, believe that you have received it, and it will be yours**."

Mark 11:24 (NIV)

> You want something but don't get it. You kill and covet, but you cannot have what you want. You quarrel and fight. **You do not have, because you do not ask God.**
>
> **James 4:2 (NIV)**

To invoke the favor of God we simply have to ask.

When talking about abundance, one of the first persons to come to mind is Joseph. By today's standards, Joseph was a billionaire, not just a millionaire. Because Joseph depended upon God, his life was totally filled with wealth of every kind, including a family with children and all the power that the Pharaoh of Egypt could give him. However, not all of Joseph's life was easy. The story of Joseph can be found in the book of Genesis, chapters 37–48. Hear the words of Joseph when he revealed himself to his brothers:

> "Do not be distressed and do not be angry with yourselves for selling me . . . God sent me ahead of you. For two years now there has been famine in the land, and for the next five years there will not be plowing and reaping. But **God sent me ahead of you to preserve for you** a remnant of earth and **to save your lives by a great deliverance**. So then, it was **not you who sent me here but God**.

He made me father to Pharaoh, lord of his entire household and ruler of all Egypt."

Genesis 45:5–8 (NIV)

Please note that God placed Joseph in a position to be blessed, all because Joseph depended upon God to lead him. Keep in mind his journey was not always filled with peace or perfection. Joseph had many adversities to fight through, but he conquered them all through his dependence upon God. In the end, Joseph was one of the most blessed human beings ever to walk the face of this earth.

Job was another example of a person that endured hardship. Through his understanding of who was in control, he found himself depending more upon God. In the end, Job achieved victory for his life. Job lost everything except his life, and God restored everything in double. Job had a larger family and possessions after his adversity than before.

After Job had prayed for his friends, the LORD made him prosperous again and gave him twice as much as he had before.

Job 42:10 (NIV)

Abundance is about having plenty of love, energy, happiness, well being, health, and friends as well as time and money. I have always yearned to be financially independent so that I did not have to worry about the future financial needs of my family and myself. I used to worry and worry about where all the money was going to come from that my family needed. In fact, all this worry and stress was probably what helped my blood pressure to increase, which was part of the reason I had a stroke at age forty-six.

You know, even after I had my stroke and realized how short life can be, I still worried about money. Never enough! It wasn't until I lost my job, after twenty-one years of service to one company and found out I had cancer, that I truly realized how harmful all those negative thoughts were to my body. I also realized that God wanted my thoughts to be on good things and on Him. It wouldn't matter how much I had planned for my family's future and my retirement, God had the ultimate control. Wow! That was an eye-opener, as they say. Let's just say that I turned my thoughts to God, and I didn't sweat the small stuff. God has a way of talking to us, and I am telling you from experience, we had better listen.

Scriptures of God's Blessings

Beloved, I wish above all things that thou **mayest prosper** and be in **health, even as thy soul prospereth.**

3 John 1:2 (KJV)

"And you, because of my blood covenant with you, I'll release your prisoners from their hopeless cells. **Come home, hope-filled prisoners**! This very day **I'm declaring a double bonus— everything you lost returned twice-over**!"

Zechariah 9:11–13 (MSG)

Yet the **LORD longs to be gracious to you; he rises to show you compassion**. For the LORD is a God of justice. Blessed are all who wait for him!

Isaiah 30:18 (NIV)

Let God be your God!

"For I know the plans I have for you," declares the LORD, "plans to **prosper** you and not to harm you, plans to give you **hope** and a future. Then you will call upon me and come and **pray to me**, and **I will listen** to you. You will seek me and find me when you **seek me with all your heart. I will be found by you,"** declares the LORD, "and will bring you back from captivity."

Jeremiah 29:11–14 (NIV)

For surely, O Lord, you bless the righteous; you surround them with **your favor as with a shield**.

Psalm 5:12 (NIV)

"The thief cometh not, but for to steal, and to kill, and to destroy: **I am come that they might have life**, and that they might have **it more abundantly**."

John 10:10 (KJV)

If they obey and serve him, they will spend the rest of their **days in prosperity and their years in contentment.**

Job 36:11 (NIV)

The fear of the LORD leads to life: Then **one rests content, untouched by trouble.**

Proverbs 19:23 (NIV)

Don't be obsessed with getting more material things. Be relaxed with what you have. Since God assured us, "I'll never let you down, never walk off and leave you," we can boldly quote, "**God is there, ready to help; I'm fearless no matter what. Who or what can get to me**?"

Hebrews 13:5 (MSG)

"Bring the whole tithe into the storehouse, that there may be food in my house. Test me in this," says the LORD Almighty, "and see if I will not t**hrow open the floodgates of heaven** and **pour out so much blessing that you will not have room enough** for it."

Malachi 3:10 (NIV)

"**Enlarge your house; build an addition. Spread out your home, and spare no expense**!"

Isaiah 54:2 (NLT)

Expect God's Favor

Our only hope in this world and the world to come is **God and Jesus Christ**. If we walk with them, they will protect us and give us a wonderful life on earth and in heaven. Let us conclude this chapter with two powerful verses that drive the point home that we must depend upon God in order for us to have victory in our lives.

> It is not for man to direct his steps.
>
> **Jeremiah 10:23 (NIV)**

> Direct my footsteps according to your word.
>
> **Psalm 119:133 (NIV)**

Steps I Took to Invoke God's Favor:

- I asked God, according to His will.
- I had faith without doubt.
- I was expectant.
- I prepared to receive.

I learned that God wanted for us to have:

- Days in prosperity and years in contentment.
- Confidence that He would never let us down, never walk off and leave us.
- So many blessings that we would not have enough room for them.
- A life, untouched by trouble.

When someone blesses you, they are invoking God's favor upon you. When I ask for God's favor, I need to be asking for all of mankind and not just myself. My true desire is that everyone comes to God and that everyone receives all of God's blessings. Let us declare our dependence upon God today and watch the tide change in our lives for the better!

Live in Victory!

Fifteen

Thank God—Praise His Name

I asked the ultimate questions:

1. How can I ever thank God enough?
2. How can I depend on God for everything?
3. How can I keep all the good things God has given me before me?
4. Do I keep all the good things God has given to me to myself?

I realized early in writing this book that I wanted to give God all the glory of my healing. I also knew that I needed to keep God's blessing before me each day. I have mentioned my healing book before. I keep, in this healing book, a list of all my blessings. As I have said before, I know beyond a shadow of a doubt that God is with me and has healed me. I must never forget this enormous blessing. When I praise God and give thanks is when I feel most empowered, because I feel connected to my Lord.

God has given us such a wonderful tool of prayer. This tool is our most powerful tool to express to the ultimate power source all our needs. This is our connector to God. Then through our faith we pull in God's energy—our source. When we praise God we are surrendering to Him, giving Him the position in our world that He deserves. When we praise Him we give Him reverence, because we fear Him and show Him the respect He has earned.

Praise Scriptures

Praise be to the God and Father of our Lord Jesus Christ, the Father of compassion and the God of all comfort.

2 Corinthians 1:3 (NIV)

David blessed GOD in full view of the entire congregation: **Blessed are you, GOD of Israel, our father** from of old and forever. To you, O GOD, belong the greatness and the might, the glory, the victory, the majesty, the splendor; **Yes! Everything in heaven, everything on earth; the kingdom all yours!** You've raised yourself high over all. **Riches and glory come from you, you're ruler over all**; You hold strength and power in the palm of your hand to build up and strengthen all. And here we are, **O God, our God, giving thanks to you, praising your splendid Name.**

1 Chronicles 29:13 (MSG)

He is your praise; he is your God, who performed for you those great and awesome wonders you saw with your own eyes.

Deuteronomy 10:21 (NIV)

Praise be to the God and Father of our Lord Jesus Christ, who has blessed us in the heavenly realms with every spiritual blessing

Ephesians 1:3 (NIV)

Thankfulness

God really does not ask a lot of me. He simply wants me to walk with Him and do what He has told me to do. One of the things He says to always keep before me is my thankfulness. Have you ever given someone a gift and they did not say thank you? I have given gifts before that went unnoticed, which really made me feel unloved to say the least. So I put that same feeling in God's perspective. When He has given me so much and I refuse to say thank you, I wonder what God thinks about me. I think He feels that maybe I do not deserve anything else until I become thankful. That is exactly what I am trying to instill in my son. To always say thank you and realize where our blessings come from.

How can I ever be thankful enough that He gave a part of Himself in Jesus Christ to come to earth and die for my sins? I can never be thankful enough. How can I ever be thankful enough when He heals me of my diseases? How can I ever be thankful enough when He supplies all my needs? On and on and on I could go! That is exactly why I keep a journal in my healing book, and each day I read over all my blessings that God has provided and write down new ones. I list all the things that I am thankful for.

Example: I am so thankful to God that He has healed me from cancer. I am going to try and pay back some of my blessings by helping others who are going through adversities like mine. That is why I will never forget where my healing and all my blessings came from—**God Almighty!**

Words from the Wise

"Much has been given us, and much will rightfully be expected from us."

—Theodore Roosevelt

Scriptures of Thanksgiving

Give thanks to the LORD, for he is good;
his love endures forever.

1 Chronicles 16:34 (NIV)

Devote yourselves to prayer, being watchful and **thankful.**

Colossians 4:2 (NIV)

Therefore, since we are receiving a kingdom that cannot be shaken, let us be **thankful**, and so worship God acceptably with reverence and awe.

Hebrews 12:28 (NIV)

And whatever you do, whether in word or deed, do it all in the name of the Lord Jesus, **giving thanks to God the Father** through him.

Colossians 3:17 (NIV)

By him therefore let us offer the **sacrifice of praise to God** continually, that is, the fruit of our lips giving thanks to his name.

Hebrews 13:15 (KJV)

Now when Daniel learned that the decree had been published, he went home to his upstairs room where the windows opened toward Jerusalem. **Three times a day he got down on his knees and prayed, giving thanks to his God, just as he had done before.**

Daniel 6:10 (NIV)

Praise the LORD. Praise God in his sanctuary; praise him in his mighty heavens. Praise him for his acts of power; praise him for his surpassing greatness. Praise him with the

sounding of the trumpet, praise him with the harp and lyre, praise him with tambourine and dancing, praise him with the strings and flute, praise him with the clash of cymbals, praise him with resounding cymbals. **Let everything that has breath praise the LORD. Praise the LORD.**

Psalm 150 (NIV)

This is our God—Praise His Name!

Then I looked, and, oh!—a door open into Heaven. The trumpet-voice, the first voice in my vision, called out, "Ascend and enter. I'll show you what happens next." I was caught up at once in deep worship and, oh!—a Throne set in Heaven with One Seated on the Throne, suffused in gem hues of amber and flame with a nimbus of emerald. Twenty-four thrones circled the Throne, with Twenty-four Elders seated, white-robed, gold-crowned. Lightning flash and thunder crash pulsed from the Throne. Seven fire-blazing torches fronted the Throne (these are the Sevenfold Spirit of God). Before the Throne it was like a clear crystal sea. Prowling around the Throne were Four Animals, all eyes. Eyes to look ahead, eyes to look behind. The first Animal like a lion, the second like an ox, the third with a human face, the fourth like an eagle in flight. The Four Animals were winged, each with six wings. They were all eyes, seeing around and within. And they chanted night and day, never taking a break:

Holy, holy, holy
Is God our Master, Sovereign-Strong,
The Was, The Is, The Coming.

Revelation 4:1–6 (MSG)

In the year that King Uzziah died, I saw the Lord seated on a throne, high and exalted, and the train of his robe filled the temple. Above him were seraphs, each with six wings: With two wings they covered their faces, with two they covered their feet, and with two they were flying. And they were calling to one another: "Holy, holy, holy is the LORD Almighty; the whole earth is full of his glory."

Isaiah 6:1–3 (NIV)

Example of His Mighty Works

The Sombrero Galaxy is found 28 million light-years from Earth. Officially called M104, this galaxy has 800 billion suns and is 50,000 light-years across.

And, isn't it interesting that we here on planet Earth think what's going on in the universe is all about us? Aren't we naive?

Now do you think God can handle anything you want or need?

God's wisdom is so deep, God's power so immense, who could take him on and come out in one piece? He moves mountains before they know what's happened, flips them on their heads on a whim. He gives the earth a good shaking up, rocks it down to its very foundations. He tells the sun, "Don't shine" and it doesn't; he pulls the blinds on the stars. All by himself he stretches out the heavens and strides on the waves of the sea. He designed the Big Dipper and Orion, the Pleiades and Alpha Centauri. We'll never comprehend all the great things he does; his miracle-surprises can't be counted.

Job 9:4–10 (MSG)

Let's give thanks to God!

Our most Holy and Righteous Father in Heaven, hallowed be thy name. I pray that the words of this book may heal people of broken hearts, broken spirits, and diseases of all kinds. We praise your name for all your glory, power, and love. We give you all the glory for all the healings each day. We thank you for all our many blessings, both spiritual and physical. We especially thank you for sending us your only begotten son. We know that you bless us because we are your children and we proclaim Christ as our Savior. We hold up the name of Yahweh above all names as our creator and father of all living things. Uphold us to always do good filled with love. Protect us from harm and evil. Fill our days with thanksgiving and prosperity. We give you thanks for all of our lives and everything we have. In Jesus Christ's Holy name I pray, Amen.

Bibliography

Allen, James. *As a Man Thinketh*. Mineola, New York: Dover Publications, 2007.

American Heart Association. *Heart Disease and Stroke Statistics—Update 2005*. Dallas, Texas: American Heart Association, 2005.

Cho, David Yonggi. *The Fourth Dimension*. Alachua, Florida: Bridge-Logos Publishers, 1979.

Cho, David Yonggi. *Unleashing the Power of Faith*. Alachua, Florida: Bridge-Logos Publishers, 2006.

Chopra, Deepak. *Quantum Healing: Exploring the Frontiers of Mind/Body Medicine*. New York: Bantam Books, 1990.

Davies, Paul. *The Mind of God: The Scientific Basis for a Rational World*. New York: Simon & Schuster, 1993.

Dyer, Wayne. *The Power of Intention*. Carlsbad, California: Hay House, Inc., 2004.

Henderson, Charles. *Self Hypnosis for the Life You Want*. Biocentrix Publishing, 2003.

Kaku, Michio. *Hyperspace: A Scientific Odyssey through Parallel Universes, Time Warps, and the 10th Dimension*. New York: Anchor, 1995.

Kehoe, John. *Mind Power into the 21st Century: Techniques to Harness the Astounding Powers of Thought*. Vancouver, BC: Zoetic Books, 1997.

McTaggart, Lynn. *The Field: The Quest for the Secret Force of the Universe*. New York: HarperCollins, 2002.

Milanovich, Norma J. and Shirley D. McCune. *The Light Shall Set You Free*. Scottsdale, Arizona: Athena Publishing, 1996.

Osteen, Joel. *Your Best Life Now: 7 Steps to Living at Your Full Potential*. Nashville, Tennessee: FaithWords, 2007.

Pickett, Joseph P. et al., eds. *The American Heritage Dictionary of the English Language*. Boston: Houghton Mifflin Company, 2000.

Price, Frederick K.C. *Answered Prayer Guaranteed!* New Kensington, Pennsylvania: Charisma House, 2006.

Robbins, Tony. *Unlimited Power: The New Science of Personal Achievement*. New York: Fireside, 1997.

Staniforth, Jeff. "How Do Affirmations Promote Vibrant Health and Well-Being?" Article originally appeared in Affirmation for the Mind newsletter. http://7stepstomentalmastery.com/healthaffirmations (accessed June 24, 2008).

Warren, Rick. *The Purpose-Driven Life*. Grand Rapids, Michigan: Zondervan, 2007.

Wicke, Roger W. "Effects of music and sound on human health." Herbalist Review, 2000, no. 1.

Acknowledgments

To all the staff at Brown Books Publishing Group whose professionalism and dedication to excellence made this book possible. A special thanks to Milli Brown and Janet Harris for believing in the book and in me.

To my loving wife Mary Beth whose inspiration helped me to finish this book.

About the Author

Wally Hogland, the son of a Christian minister, was born in Ft. Smith, Arkansas, and raised in Greenville, Texas. He is a graduate of Texas A&M Commerce and currently lives in Rowlett, Texas, with his wife Mary Beth and son Brandon.

Wally enjoys playing tennis and is presently working on his professional certification in the sport. He never imagined that he would survive both a stroke and cancer and live to tell about it. Now, he can say he has survived some of the most amazing adversities a human being can describe.

Second Chance for Life is his personal story of managing and conquering the difficult challenges he faced. He maintains the belief that victory in this life is for the taking, if one follows certain guidelines.

God bless.